Praise for Endless Encores

♩ ♩ ♩

"From *Carmen Sandiego* to Disney Online to Shop.com to his first book *This Is Rage*, Ken Goldstein knows about reinvention. Now he has written a parable with insight, charm, and authority."
— Michael Eisner, CEO, The Tornante Company and Author of *Working Together*

"My creative energies are renewed by Ken Goldstein's *Endless Encores*. My highest and most sincere praise for Mr. Goldstein is that it becomes difficult to sit down while reading his engaging book. The dialogue has the organic effect of making me want to jump up and get into action—and into the business of inspiring new possibilities. The brilliance of the ideas in *Endless Encores* is that they strike us, simultaneously, as gloriously revolutionary, and—in the Socratic way—as something we knew in our guts all along. In my work as a conductor, my challenge is to lead artists and audiences into a new and transformative experience with every fresh listening—even when the music is familiar. Mr. Goldstein offers profound lessons and an inspiring roadmap to achieving transcendent and unexpected results. This is essential reading for anyone who is serious about leadership and creating real change."
— Rachael Worby, Artistic Director/Music Director, MUSE/IQUE

"Ken Goldstein has penned an insightful new book that demonstrates the power of people, products, and profits. It's an important tool for managers in all organizations who wish to lead their organization to new heights. Most intriguing, it is written as a fictional dialogue between a successful CEO and a manager besieged with troubles. Their Socratic interaction pulls you in and keeps you reading. It's an invaluable dialogue that you must have."
— Gene Del Vecchio, USC Marshall School of Business

"Ken Goldstein has written an inspiring, empowering book that encourages each of us to aspire to the extraordinary—to be exceptional listeners and amazing thinkers—and understand that in the process of reinvention, we can all find our own *Endless Encores*. In *Endless Encores*, Ken generously shares his own notebook for repeated success, vividly demonstrating the power of people, products, and profits while underscoring the importance of resilience and continuous reinvention."
— Barb Adams, Talk Host, *Amerika Now*, Genesis Communications Network

"Bravo! Ken Goldstein is a true maestro at building, supporting, and directing highly talented creative and technical teams. Brilliant in its simplicity, *Endless Encores* explores the central, overriding importance of people in today's complex, Internet-driven global economy. The conversational narrative is an easily accessible device for him to share the secret of his success. A must read for all creative executives."
— Christopher Keefe, Chief Marketing Officer, Omidyar Network

"In this delightful narrative, Ken Goldstein explains how managers can create the right conditions in their own business line to make it more likely that profitable products will emerge. And the best reward is a simple list of questions that reveal whether you are on track to do so. I intend to ask them of myself regularly!"
— Emily Smith, President and GM, Media, Brit + Co

"Great read! Compelling message and great reminder for all leaders. *Endless Encores* is delightful and presents critical lessons for every leader. It is the kind of book we should pick up every now and then. This book helps you refocus."
— Patricia Wilson, Executive Director/CEO, Make-A-Wish Greater Bay Area

"Full of hard-won business lessons, presented in a delightful and accessible style, Ken Goldstein's latest is both fun to read and full of valuable insights. The deeper truths about blending creative ideals and practical production realities resonated with my own experiences, clearly the result of a lot of trial by combat on Goldstein's part."
— Noah Falstein, Chief Game Designer, Google

"Drawing on his experience as a team manager, CEO, and coach, Goldstein says, 'Sometimes you have to give people what they don't even know they want yet.' In his book *Endless Encores*, he has given us an insightful, highly relevant, and easy-to-read guide for anyone who has to work with other human beings. Along with my iPhone, I will carry its simple wisdom and inspiring business leadership advice with me everywhere I go."
— Irv Rothenberg, CPA/PFS; Principal, Buckingham Family of Financial Services

"I couldn't put this book down! Ken Goldstein has written a next-gen business parable that puts the pursuit of success into perspective. It's a book I'll share with colleagues—and keep a copy for future insights."
— Beth Collins Ellard, EVP Media, The Advertising Council

"Ken Goldstein has tackled important business issues in an entertaining format. This deceptively easy to read story has important lessons on leadership, courage, and resilience. It is written as a dialogue between a manager at the beginning of his career and a CEO nearing the end of hers. The manager exhibits the first quality he will need to move from being an individual contributor to a leader by self-awareness of his strengths and weaknesses. The qualities needed to be a good leader— including flexibility, enterprise-wide thinking, engaging and motivating strong team members— are explored and written in a manner that makes you think back to the topics again and again. Goldstein calls upon his own experience as a CEO to add authenticity to the topics."
— Becky Stein, Senior Client Partner, Korn Ferry

"Ken Goldstein has done a masterful job in outlining the importance of making great people decisions and how it impacts leadership as well as the development of a great company. If you follow his advice in *Endless Encores*, you will have the tools to be a great leader."
— Robert F. Myers, EVP Development, Hathaway-Sycamores Child & Family Services

"Ken Goldstein's delightful and engaging parable drew me into the center of the story and I felt as if I was experiencing it firsthand. I was simultaneously cheering with each vital insight as he brought them together in a simple yet thought-provoking guide to people, products, and profits. Mr. Goldstein's *Endless Encores* is an important book for the critical steps to positive development and growth as an individual, team, or company. I learned important steps for my own future growth reading this book. If you want to have a career rather than a job, I suggest you do the same."
— Mary-Margaret Walker, Educator & Career Specialist, Mary-Margaret Network

"Dating back to Socrates, the arts have provided memorable examples of teachers we all wish we encountered at some point along the journey of life who make us question our thinking and seek answers that might be right in front of us. Ken Goldstein has modestly created a fictional persona in Daphne and her charming, selfless encounter with Paul—a brief but powerful lesson that will last a lifetime. *Endless Encores* invites the reader to be a fly on the wall for their dialogue and chart a course for their own professional journey with the simple but powerful formula shared."
— Dan Sherlock, former President, Cinedigm Software and Baseline, Inc.

Endless Encores

Repeating Success Through People, Products, and Profits

♩ ♩ ♩

A Business Parable by

Ken Goldstein

The Story Plant
Studio Digital CT, LLC
PO Box 4331
Stamford, CT 06907

Print ISBN-13: 978-1-61188-208-7
E-book ISBN-13: 978-1-936558-68-1

Visit our website at www.thestoryplant.com
Visit the author's blog at www.corporateintel.us
Follow the author on Twitter @CorporateIntel

First Story Plant Hardcover Printing: September 2015
Printed in the United States of America
9 8 7 6 5 4 3 2 1

Contents

♩ ♩ ♩

For Padre David Coon

A guy who never did the for-profit thing.

But boy did he know how to sell and get us to be
our best.

Preface

♪ ♪ ♪

When I finished writing my first novel, *This Is Rage*, I thought I would take a break from fiction and pull together a "Best Of" collection of the many blog entries I had written about business over the years. I started my blog when I started my first book, and I wrote them in parallel to distract myself from digging in too hard on any one passage without breathing room to evolve. When I embarked on this book, I didn't want to write just another book on business leadership. The world had plenty of those, among my favorites and often most quoted, *Only the Paranoid Survive* by Andrew Grove, *Built to Last* and *Good to Great* by Jim Collins, and *First Break All the Rules* by Marcus Buckingham and Curt Coffman.

To solve the issue of the ordinary, I decided I would write a wraparound story that would tie the blog entries together as a whole and differentiate the collection from what I had already published to the cloud for free. As I played around with inventing the characters and voices of Daphne and Paul, I found my direction shifting from nonfiction back to fiction, which felt lively and natural, and fit nicely with the world view of my publisher, The Story Plant.

Then two things happened. If you've ever gone on the writing journey yourself, you know *at least* two bends in the metal are to be expected. You just don't know when or where to expect them.

First, as I embraced the full ethos of what I was writing, the idea of a "Best Of" collection started to bother me. The whole premise of this book was how to go from one project to the next without getting bogged down, and here I was mining my own archive material for a follow-up. The argument was undermined by its own antithetical construct. So I wanted to bag it.

Second, as I came to layer the realities and eccentricities of Daphne and Paul, they became real characters in a grounded story that I believed could stand on its own. Maybe because they were new and the posts were old, I gravitated to the new, where I always find hope. I sent some early sketches to my deeply admired editor, Lou Aronica, and said, "What do you think? Can we do it without the expository?" To which he replied, "I think you answered your own question—there's a new story of its own here, so tell it."

And here we are.

The heart of this book emerged in a blog post I wrote several years ago called "Dodging the Greatest Hits Graveyard." At one time I thought that might become the book's title, the core idea of which came into my mind at a live performance by Trans-Siberian Orchestra. My wife and I are regulars whenever TSO tours, and if you have never seen one of their holiday shows, it is almost impossible to describe the mix of hammering guitar chords, electronic violins, big hair rock progressions, clamoring distortion, acoustic classical and jazz leitmotifs, lasers, fireworks, indoor snow, musicians flying on swivel cranes over the stage, and spoken word storytelling. TSO fans are avid, but at every show the band makes the point of introducing new material, however unfamiliar to the crowd it might be. The courage to debut the unknown in front of adoring, expectant followers struck me not only as emblematic of continuing success, but necessary and vital to win in the present while seeding the future. Hey, it worked for Beethoven and Mozart.

I always wanted to expand that blog post into a bigger idea: the bravery to go against the grain and offer an audience something they might not otherwise have welcomed at the moment. This was not foreign terrain to me. I used to watch exceptionally creative people on my own teams struggle with follow-up success, some better than others. It was always an awful, painful occurrence, filled with doubt, questioning, and worry that their last work really might be "their last work." I wondered how hard it must have been for the Eagles to go back into the studio after *Hotel California* and record *The Long Run*. I wondered how Tom Wolfe could find his way back to the typewriter after *The Right Stuff*, and then again after *The Bonfire of the Vanities*. I wondered how Steve Jobs could launch the most iconic consumer technology company of our lifetime, get fired shortly after the success of the Mac, then return years later and reinvent the music business, the mobile phone business, and the handheld computer business one after another in a single decade. I wondered if there might be a way to help others push themselves through the process of reinvention.

I still wonder that.

In the following pages I will tell you a story and ask that you take from it what works for you. At the end of each chapter, I suggest you jot down some big-picture questions that occur to you while you are reading, perhaps expanding on the summary points suggested. Note that I am suggesting you capture questions, not answers. We all answer tough questions in our own way, and that's what makes us unique in how we approach the world, but perhaps the questions are something we share. When you get to the end of the book, there's a short but important pop quiz (please don't peek!). If some of my questions there align with the ones you are asking yourself, then we have landed on shared ground. Should you find yourself hungry for more material to inspire questions, we've also zipped up the relevant blog posts I originally thought about including in this book into a single, convenient eBook collection you can download free at TheStoryPlant.com.

Until then allow me to share this story and let you think about it. If it helps you sort through some of your own questions, drop me a line and let me know. All of this comes from on-the-job experience, where I am confident a lot of the people who lived it with me have embraced the ideals as a path to continuity and resilience. I wish for you the same, and a lifetime of success defined as only you can define it, but never a one-hit wonder.

Los Angeles, California
Spring 2015

We got time to think of the ones we love
While the miles roll away
But the only time that seems too short
Is the time that we get to play

— Jackson Browne, "The Load Out"

♩ ♩ ♩

Chapter 1: One Night in an Airport Lounge

♩ ♩ ♩

Success is nearly impossible to repeat. No one wins all the time. It's often the case that a company's hit product is followed up by a mediocre one. Don't feel bad. We see this every day.

Paul couldn't get those words out of his head. As he sat at the corner of the bar in the San Francisco International Airport executive lounge popping pretzels into his mouth, his fate was all but sealed. He had enjoyed an amazing three years. He was on his game, on top of the world. Now it seemed there was only one place to go. He didn't want to go there, but all at once he realized the odds were against him.

With the announcement that his flight home to Los Angeles would be delayed another two hours after the last two-hour delay, Paul ordered another glass of the house red. He knew he had blown it booking a corridor flight out of SFO on a summer Friday with the normal fog and weekend exit rush, but that was the price for not wanting to sit in traffic on the Bay Bridge to Oakland. Another bad decision, he thought, however small. He wondered how many other bad decisions he had recently made without knowing it, and when he would find out. The wine should have been improving his mood, but it never quite worked the way he wanted it. Like sales figures, the impact of a glass of wine was impossible to predict. A lot depended on timing.

It had been an eye-opening few days for him. He had come to San Francisco at company expense to preview his team's new product for the industry press. The public relations department had booked a non-stop lineup of interviews to demo the new work in advance of its planned release a few short weeks in the future. Product sales from his prior release were still skyrocketing and showed no signs of cresting. That groundbreaker, launched a full three years ago, had changed his career forever. He had been promoted to VP of Product Development following glowing accolades from peers and competitors. He had been celebrated widely as a rising star to be watched, and catapulted to a high-profile series of public speaking appearances in rooms filled with talented job seekers all wanting to join his team.

Problem was, all those conference talks ended with the same question: What are you going to launch next?

Paul had just delivered the answer to that question in the form of his next big thing, admittedly in beta, but far enough along to illustrate its full spectrum of features and benefits. The press had yawned. This was not what Paul had expected. No, not at all.

🎤 "What are you going to launch next?"

Had the last one been lightning in a bottle, he wondered. Were the accolades all behind him, a modest footnote of triumph turned ancient history? He had seen enough brazen colleagues come and go in a single product cycle to know every product required a new commitment—that being able to start over without hesitation separated the real winners from the forgettables. Next up he would have to show the product to the retail accounts for presales, and he knew the flat buzz from this press tour would inescapably precede him. He didn't know where to go from here, and that was a scary place to be.

Paul barely noticed when a woman, apparently in her mid-sixties, took the other corner seat beside him. His face was buried in his mobile phone, scrolling through alternative flights to connect through other cities, none of which were likely to get him home sooner. She was well dressed and trim, her shoulder-length hair in perfect order but, at twice his age, a bit imperial. For all he knew, she was just another executive at the bar ordering a drink. Her taste was Scotch.

"What's the matter?" she asked without invitation. "The look on your face tells me it's something more than the delayed flight."

"It's the delayed flight," he said, scowling at the mobile screen that offered no more news than the flight to LAX was now TBD. That would be the last flight of the night. If it went, it went. If it didn't, the next one would be in the morning.

"I checked with the gate agent. They're saying fifty/fifty for LAX," she said.

"How did you know I was going to LA?" he asked.

"Lucky guess," she said. "I'm pretty good at reading people. My name is Daphne."

"I'm Paul Beckett. They told you fifty/fifty? Sounds more like seventy-five/twenty-five against."

"You're not much of an optimist, are you, Paul?" replied Daphne. "The equipment is at the gate, but they wouldn't say what was wrong with it. They offered me the chance to rebook to an early morning flight with hotel on the house. I'm sure they'd offer you the same."

"I'll take my chances until they cancel," said Paul. "I need to get home."

"Family commitment?" asked Daphne.

"No, I'm not married. Maybe someday. I have to rescue this new project I botched before we release it. I'm not sure how we're going to fix it."

"I've been to that launch party," relayed Daphne. "Are you having a bad year?"

Paul wasn't sure why she was asking him so many questions. He hadn't been in the mood to talk, but suddenly he found the words emptying out of him.

"No, actually I've been having a stellar year," answered Paul. "Three good years to tell you the truth. Three amazing years. We created this new videogame three years ago. It's stayed in the top ten since its first week on the charts, which doesn't happen often."

"That sounds tremendously exciting," said Daphne. "I don't know anything about videogames, but I do know when they are hits, they make a lot of money for the people who produce them."

"Yes, barrels of cash delivered without delay to the front door," said Paul. "I got a big bonus, stock options, and they promoted me to vice president. A year before the release, I was a lowly product manager living in a small apartment and driving a ten-year-old junk heap. Six months later I bought a condo with a view and a cool new hybrid."

"A bounty of treasure, yet you're staring at your sour reflection in a glass of cheap red wine," commented Daphne. "It doesn't add up."

"Do you always offer barstool psychotherapy to strangers in airport clubs?" Paul wasn't quite sure how this conversation had begun or how she had gotten him to open up so quickly, but Daphne had an impressive presence and seemed to know a bit about business.

"I've figured out that flight delays go a lot more quickly with good conversation," laughed Daphne. "Long flights, too."

"What do you do?" inquired Paul.

"I'm with an electronics component company here in the Bay Area," replied Daphne. "We manufacture the less visible elements of circuit boards. I came in with the turnaround team about a decade ago—a few years after the company went public and then got crushed by overpromising Wall Street. I wasn't sure we could resuscitate this one, but I saw pockets of strength hiding in the shadows and I was up for the challenge. We got most of the things that matter aligned and the stock recovered nicely."

"Sounds like you know what you're doing," said Paul. "I wish I had your confidence."

"I've had my ups and downs, like everyone in business," offered Daphne. "I've learned a few things along the way, and it certainly hasn't been a cakewalk. In this last job, a lot went right for me, but I think it might be time to do something else. Follow-ups are hard, but reinvention keeps your thinking fresh. Change is always on my mind, certainly at the moment."

"I can't imagine giving up my job, not willingly," gasped Paul. "You really are confident."

"A job is never yours to give up," said Daphne. "It's a box on an organization chart you fill for a while, until someone else fills it, or until the company goes away. It ends when it's time."

"I don't get it—how is it not my job?" asked Paul doubtingly.

"If you don't own the company, it's their job, not yours. They lease it to you for a while for the value you create beyond what you cost. At the end of the lease, if you paid off the tab and have more valuable knowledge and skills than you had when you signed on, it's a good deal for everyone. If you take their money but don't get better at what you do, you got burned."

"That's a scary way of looking at the business world," stated Paul.

"The alternative is to go out on your own, but of course that comes with its own set of costs. There's

🎙 "A job is never yours to give up."

no easy way to stay in the game. If you're looking for certainty or shortcuts, forget it."

Paul looked Daphne in the eye and tried to make sense of what she was saying. She seemed to know something he didn't know, but did it matter? The few extra decades of experience she had on him had brought some wisdom, yet their conversation was a bit circular and it was making him uncomfortable. As she suddenly pushed back her barstool and began to step away, he saw the exit opportunity he needed to make the coming hours more productive. At the same time he felt like he might be losing the answer he needed before he even asked the question. If only he knew what the question was.

"This flight is outbound for me, another weekend on the road," said Daphne. "I need to step away for a moment. Okay if I leave my drink here and we continue our conversation in a few moments?"

"I'm not going anywhere," blurted out Paul.

They both laughed at that. As Daphne walked off toward the restroom, Paul felt a sense of calm. Perhaps he hadn't driven her to a more curious conversation elsewhere in the waiting room. He returned his gaze to his smartphone, just as the bartender interrupted him with a probing glance. He was a burly, ageless attendant in need of a diet and a shave, the worn vest and angled bow tie affixed to his frame awarded him home-field confidence and authority.

"You do know who you're schmoozing with there?" prompted the bartender. "Daphne Lonner?"

"A rather interesting lady," replied Paul, looking for the absent nametag where it should have been on the bartender's lapel. "She's smart and kind, very open. Good enough way to pass a little time. Is she a regular here?"

"Google her," directed the bartender, as if Paul had missed the point entirely.

Paul ran a quick query on his smartphone: Daphne Lonner. His eyes practically popped out his skull as he looked up from the small screen.

"She's like a billionaire," said Paul. "She's taken four companies public and has sixty-eight technology patents in her own name. She has about forty thousand people working for her at this very moment."

"Maybe not a billionaire yet, but I'll bet you a year's worth of tips she'll retire one," said the bartender. "Maybe you should pay closer attention when she talks. I guess that's up to you."

"Not taking that bet, but thanks for the heads up," responded Paul.

When Daphne returned, she resumed the conversation as if there hadn't been a single second of interlude. "I think I know what's bothering you," she said, taking her seat again at the bar.

Paul was silent. He couldn't believe he was having drinks with a CEO billionaire. Once he deciphered who Daphne was, he was sure she was going to ditch him for better company. That obviously wasn't her style. She wasn't even flying on a private jet. He thought about what the bartender had tossed off in passing—that he should listen more closely to what she was saying. This was a once-in-a-lifetime opportunity to learn.

"Did Harold tell you to Google me?" asked Daphne, noting Paul's tentativeness. Paul nodded like a school kid responding to a surprise drill. Harold-the-bartender burst out laughing and straightened his tie. Daphne looked at him pryingly and shook her head, but she didn't seem all that bothered. She took in the moment and rolled to the next. "Paul, you think perhaps you were luckier than you were smart, and now you're wondering if your luck has run out. Is that it?"

"I think you're right," confirmed Paul. "I might have gotten lucky on the hit game. The two I produced before it had sub-measurable sales. Then out of nowhere, we have a gigantic hit."

"That's when everyone started looking at you like you knew what you were doing, and you weren't sure you had a clue what to do next."

"And now I may have a duck on my hands," added Paul. "A duck that quacks off key, just like the two bombs before it. Well, maybe not that bad. It's an okay product, but maybe I should have pushed harder. After a hit, a B is an F."

"Endless Encores," remarked Daphne, again catching Paul off guard.

"What do you mean by that?" asked Paul, intrigued but not fully following.

"Do you like music?" asked Daphne. "Contemporary bands, classic rock, pop tunes from various times?"

"Sure, of course," said Paul. "Who doesn't have a favorite band or two?"

"Those bands that are your favorites—did they have one or two hits, or a pretty decent run over the years?"

"You mean like the Eagles? The Rolling Stones? The Beatles? Obviously they had a string of hits, sometimes one after another."

"How hard do you think it was for them to keep trying to top themselves?" asked Daphne.

"Hard," conveyed Paul. "Very, very hard. In my business, hardly anyone repeats."

"More like the one-hit wonders on the pop charts from the sixties, seventies, and eighties," noted Daphne. "'My Sharona.' 'Tainted Love.' 'Kung Fu Fighting.' 'Video Killed the Radio Star.'"

"You're dating yourself a little," chuckled Paul. "But yes, you nailed it. I don't want to be a one-hit wonder. I don't want to be like Friendster or Pet Rocks or the Cabbage Patch Kids. I want to make lots of hits, like you said, an endless series of hits. I want to be that guy. How do you make hits time after time after time?"

"A lot of us ask ourselves that question," shared Daphne. "I wish I could tell you the answer. What I can tell you is that luck is not such a bad thing. It's okay to embrace it."

"Yeah, but can you repeat it?" asked Paul. "Can you make it happen again and again, predict it, make it repeatable?"

"From my experience, I think the best you can do is increase your odds. To build a career that allows for Endless Encores, you can never stand on your laurels. You have to be innovating all the time, not just when the clock is ticking against you. You do a little crowd pleasing with what they know, then a little thought leading by showing them something new."

"It would be difficult to think about Endless Encores with a limited repertoire," noted Paul.

"The only sure path to a limited repertoire is not to push yourself beyond the familiar. Your range is only gated by your courage to pursue the unknown, despite the doubters who relish the false safety of narrowing your path. You risk, you stretch, you can't know what's going to stick. No matter how much you know the familiar will carry you, you navigate the balance of old and new, constantly committing to reinvention. Repeat success is getting comfortable with the uncomfortable, knowing that luck will shine again, but never knowing when or how."

"And then you fail anyway," said Paul, motioning for the too-clever bartender to bring him another glass. "If you as the CEO don't know how to do it, what can I do to create an endless string of hits?"

"You make sure you are always trying the untried, no matter how much your customers want what is already working for them," answered Daphne. "Sometimes you have to give people what they don't even know they want yet. Your fans think they only want to hear your hits, but that's a trap. If all you give them is what they know, you never again have the chance to debut the unknown. That risk is the only way you can expand your catalogue."

🎤 "You risk, you stretch, you can't know what's going to stick."

"You sound more like a music agent than a tech geek," said Paul.

"What was the name of your hit game?" asked Daphne.

"Ethereal Gaze," answered Paul proudly. "It's a journey through a mirrored galaxy, where you bring peace in place of war and nurture civilizations with diplomacy instead of weaponry."

"I've actually heard of that," said Daphne. "It was a breakthrough visually if I remember, and without much shooting."

"No shooting at all," qualified Paul. "When we brought it to market, people thought we were nuts. When we saw a little movement and doubled down on the advertising budget, they were certain we had lost our minds. Sales were beyond belief, almost impossible to imagine."

"How about that, I don't even play videogames and I've heard of your hit. You cut through the noise. You created a brand. What's the name of the game you just showed to the press?"

"Ethereal Gaze 2: The Unseating," declared Paul. "The theme is what happens when we discover that much of what we believe doesn't fly in the face of corruption."

"Sounds a tad derivative," surmised Daphne. "Maybe a little battle slipped in?"

"The fans asked for combat mode in the focus tests after the first game," replied Paul. "Our business is built on sequels, and we listen to customer feedback carefully. We try to give people what they want. Like you suggested, we think in terms of brands and brand extensions. A franchise is a property than can be replicated. Isn't that the safest bet?"

"It's half a bet," explained Daphne. "How far into the unknown did you push your team? Did you break any new ground, give your customers reason to be excited about the sequel?"

"Maybe not as much as we could have," admitted Paul. "Hence the yawn."

"I'm not telling you to ignore your base," said Daphne. "Sometimes people think they know what they want, but what they really want is to be surprised and delighted, and there isn't a roadmap for that. When I go to a Rolling Stones concert, of course I want to hear 'Satisfaction,' 'Jumping Jack Flash,' and 'Gimme Shelter.' But if they don't play anything new that intrigues me, I might as well stay home and listen to the recordings I already have."

"I get it, but that new stuff is impossible to predict in a vacuum, and most of it gets ignored," said Paul.

Daphne picked up her glass and swirled it with a grin. "You took an immense chance with *Ethereal Gaze* and it delivered for you. You've had a good long drink from the well, so you know what that's like."

"Right, but how do you know what to try after that, without embarrassing yourself and everyone around you? My boss thinks I know something, and I really don't. I have him fooled completely and as soon as we bring out this game, he'll probably find out."

"Is he a good boss?" asked Daphne. "I mean, not perfect, but a decent fellow?"

"Well, he promoted me, so he can't be all bad. Yeah, he's okay. Not perfect, but okay."

"I think you'll be fine," said Daphne, setting down her glass after a poised sip. "I don't know if you can make your next game a hit, or the one after that. But I do have a few ideas that I think can help you improve your chances, if you don't mind listening to a few war stories."

"We have a two-hour flight delay, at least," said Paul. "I've heard that good conversation can make the time fly."

Daphne pushed back her glass and smiled again. "You see, there's hidden opportunity in every mishap. You just have to look for it."

Paul looked around the fluorescent-lit room. Everyone had tired eyes. He and Daphne weren't the only ones stuck at the airport on a Friday evening. Not surprisingly, no one looked back at him. Everyone had issues of their own consuming them; so many faces buried in laptops and tablets and mobile phones. A few had taken to light conversation, and Paul wondered if anyone in the room might be having a discussion similar to the one he was having with Daphne. It was impossible to tell. It was also impossible to internalize all that Daphne was saying. He thought he might be missing the point, but most of all he wanted to stop feeling that for the rest of his career he would be walking on thin ice. Everyone in that airport lounge had notched a few wins and many losses. Were they all as afraid as he was of admitting that?

It suddenly occurred to Paul that Daphne hadn't told him anything he didn't already know. Of course he needed a constant stream of new products to test, sequels as well as new ideas, but she hadn't reduced his risk beyond not trying at all. That left him with no competitive advantage over anyone in that lounge or the outside world. It was an honorable enough manifesto, but not particularly actionable. Now he was on edge.

"You haven't gone beyond the obvious," exclaimed Paul. "Continue to launch unproven products all the time while harvesting existing successes. So what? You haven't told me how. That's what makes a difference, knowing how to create winners consistently. Do you have a formula for that?"

"Not a formula, but an approach, a methodology that works for me and my team," continued Daphne. "Actually it's more of a loose construct than a methodology, but I'll be happy to share it with you."

"A loose construct," echoed Paul. "My lucky day. Bring it on."

"Are you listening or putting up a wall?" returned Daphne.

"Sorry, that was rude," apologized Paul. "Can you just tell me what I should be doing?"

"In a moment, but first I want you to understand that product releases only seem like endpoints. That can be deceptive, even unnerving. The products we bring to market don't exist in isolation. They are part of the sine curve that maps your career, the overlapping highs and lows, the peaks and pits. Funny enough, only a few products will define your career. The rest you'll forget, but you're much more likely to remember the people who worked closely with you on all of them."

"Sounds sensible enough," said Paul. "Okay, keep making me a believer."

"You said you were a product manager before. Now you're in the executive ranks. What do you think has changed for you?"

"I guess the title means people have to listen to me now," answered Paul.

"Forgive me, Paul, and I do get a little abrupt from time to time, but titles don't mean a damn thing. Your boss can give you a title. Your boss can't make people listen to you. You have to earn that. It doesn't sound like you get that yet."

There was an awkward stretch of silence. Daphne's tone had shifted. Suddenly he saw the CEO in her. He wasn't sure if he wanted to hear more, but she continued anyway.

"I think I may have jumped forward to the punchline," conveyed Daphne. "We'll come back later to what has changed for you. Instead, let me ask you as simply as I can: What do you think is the key to getting your next big hit?"

"Lots of people buying it," quipped Paul. "Broad distribution, smart marketing, developing something that people want."

"Yes, good marketing does help mediocre products fail faster and more spectacularly," replied Daphne. "How about something less obvious? Tell

🎤 "The products we bring to market don't exist in isolation."

me about your management philosophy, especially now that you're officially part of the *Dilbert* brass."

"I don't think I have one," uttered Paul.

"Sure you do. You might have had your one big hit to date by accident, but I don't think you became VP by accident. What got you there?"

"I made a lot of money for my company," asserted Paul.

"Don't make me give up and book a ride on the train," rebuked Daphne. "Tell me, what is it you do as a videogame maker?"

"We make stuff."

"A clear enough answer—you said 'we,' which is a good sign. Who is *we*? Who makes the stuff?"

"Our teams do the work," answered Paul. "The employees and contractors we hire. Our people. And they're good at it. Really, really good."

"There you go," said Daphne. "Your good people make the stuff. What kind of stuff?"

"I don't know, wacky, creative stuff," said Paul. "Products that engage the imagination of our customers."

"People make the products," summarized Daphne. "Then what happens?"

Paul should have known the answer, but he didn't. This was going to be obvious, and he couldn't pull it out of a hat.

"If your business model is sound, your company makes money," said Daphne. "The part you said that got you promoted. Profits."

"I had an inkling that was what you were going to say," replied Paul. "I thought it might be a trick question."

"No tricks," said Daphne. "That's my business philosophy, and it's simple. People, Products, Profits—in that order."

"Shouldn't a business figure out how it is going to make money first?" asked Paul.

"Yes, of course. I gave you the correct order to make that happen, at least for me. I've been at this four decades, a survivor of many trends, a lot of bombs, and just enough wins to pay the bills and start the cycle anew."

"That little saying is what's going to keep my career on a path to Endless Encores?"

"No, not really. You're going to need all that luck we talked about," said Daphne. "You want a shot at luck? You want a shot at a string of successes? My playbook tells me it's more than a little saying."

"People, Products, Profits—in that order?"

"Yes, and since there's no word on our flight, let's dig in a little, shall we?"

"Do you mind if I jot down a few notes as we go?" asked Paul. "I want to make sure I encode all this stuff for later recall."

Paul reached for his mobile and opened up a blank page in a note-taking app. Daphne gently motioned for him to put it away, then reached in her shoulder bag and handed Paul a small spiral-bound notebook emblazoned with her company's logo.

🎤 "People, Products, Profits—in that order."

SalientCorp. "Take this, it will give you something to remember our conversation," said Daphne. "Perhaps it's a little analog, but if you don't lose it, it will never become obsolete because of technology."

Paul closed his mobile and took the notebook. A gleaming chrome pen was attached to the spine with Velcro. He opened the cover and wrote the date on the first page. He also wrote Daphne's name and the letters *SFO*. It was the best way he knew how to begin.

"Are you really planning to quit being a CEO?" asked Paul, somewhat skeptically.

"We'll get to that soon enough," said Daphne. "I think we can both learn a lot here. Neither of us is big on losing, and that's a promising place to start. Let's see where the notes take us."

"Should I expect a test at the end?" joked Paul.

"More like a pop quiz," affirmed Daphne. "It should come when you least expect it."

♩ ♩ ♩

Paul's Notebook: One Night in an Airport Lounge

♫ ♫ ♫

♪ All success resets expectations for what comes next.

♪ An opportunity is much more valuable than a job.

♪ Offer customers more than what they think they want.

♪ Leadership is earned and recognized, not granted.

♪ People make products, which when successful create profits.

Chapter 2: People

♩ ♩ ♩

It was getting late in the evening, and as yet there was no additional update on the flight departures. At this point Paul was sort of hoping it would go that way. To leave this conversation unfinished was not something that held much appeal.

"What don't I know that I wish I knew?" asked Paul, knowing that didn't exactly come out right. "We put everything into this new game, everything we had to give, but the end result isn't flourishing."

"Seems like we're making quick progress with that wall," prodded Daphne. "The truth is, you already know everything you need to know. All I can do is perhaps get you to rethink it in a different context. Take me through the project from the beginning."

"The good one or the follow-up?" asked Paul.

"Why would I want to retrace the path of mediocrity?" replied Daphne. "The good one, the big winner—where did you begin with the original *Ethereal Gaze*?"

"We started with a pitch. We'd been kicking around this concept for a few years, the idea of an enormous war game, galactic in scope, but without a lot of weapons—without any bullets, or tactical bombs, or spleens exploding—any of the normal shooter stuff that was leaping off the shelf. We said we'd try to do it with clever ideas of strategy, mind-blowing graphics, a full symphonic soundtrack, and characters that made you believe they were real."

"Sounds visionary, heck of an agenda for a library of program code," lauded Daphne. "You even went against the grain and tried to build something that wasn't a proven big seller. But tell me, and I sort of asked you this before but it is worth repeating, who is *we*?"

"We, the team," answered Paul. "The core design group, the people I see every day who completely know this stuff, who come up with the ideas that make it happen."

"Cool, got it. Then let me ask you, which came first, the concept, or the talent to create it?"

"Why do I think this is another trick question?" asked Paul.

"The last time you thought I asked you a trick question it wasn't, so go with your instinct. Which comes first, the idea, or those who offer the idea? This is a key starting point, kind of like the chicken and egg thing, only we're going to solve it."

"You can't have an idea without someone expressing it," said Paul, hoping he hadn't said something too obvious.

"There you have it, bulls-eye," declared Daphne. "Not just someone expressing it; someone with the ability and training to express it, and then be able to deliver on it. A team or an individual, it doesn't matter. The foundation is the same. Let's talk a little about talent."

"I'll try to keep up with you," remarked Paul. "You have a lot of big ideas."

"Too many people I've encountered over the years in business think it's solely the big idea that matters," continued Daphne. "Don't get me wrong, big ideas are critical to success. You need spectacular concepts when you envision new products and services you want to bring to market. We'll talk about that shortly. But before you can even think about creating, marketing, distributing, and selling anything of value, you have to have the right people in place to get the job done. Desperate leaders spend too much time worrying first about output. Long-term leaders spend the majority of their time thinking about talent."

"I don't know about that," replied Paul. "I live in a world where customers need to be hugely excited, almost frothing at the mouth, standing in line overnight outside the store, waiting for the product to release before it's even on the shelf."

"Don't flatter yourself. In one way or another, we all do," countered Daphne. "Great ideas can be thrilling, but they don't make payroll. Ideas get the ball rolling, but they are overrated. We worry too much about those who would steal them. Getting a product to market that embodies a great idea is what matters, and that is extraordinarily difficult. Products don't build themselves."

🎤 "Long-term leaders spend the majority of their time thinking about talent."

"Proven time and again. We've all been there," said Paul. "If the idea doesn't get made, it's vaporware. Execution is what matters. You win again."

"We all win when we get the right people onboard," said Daphne. "The long-term leader reveres talent. The long-term leader also knows the word *talent* is applied much too loosely and bandied about without enough vetting. What do you think talent is?"

Paul knew enough about Daphne's style at this point to answer in a straightforward manner. "It's what people are good at doing, right?"

"Sort of, but *good* is a tough word to wrap your head around. How about *extraordinary*?"

"Extraordinary is pretty far reaching," said Paul. "Everyone can't be extraordinary, otherwise there is no such thing. You'd hire so few people, you'd never get anything done."

"Yes, that's mostly right, but extraordinary can be aspirational," added Daphne. "That kind of aspiration is exactly what you want on your team. Extraordinary people want to work with other extraordinary people and consistently aspire to triumph over sameness. It's less about being gifted, and more about never leaving any high-value energy uncaptured."

"Are you suggesting that winning teams self-select?" asked Paul.

"Yes. Talent knows the opposite of the extraordinary is mediocrity, and will never allow cycles to be wasted on sloppy thinking or execution. Real talent harnesses what it has and unlocks what it doesn't. There is natural ability, there is the discipline that develops natural ability, there is the unending study of one's craft, and there is the exponential lifting of performance by the selfless combination of efforts."

"It sounds like you're saying that if the work environment isn't right, talent can be squandered," replied Paul. "The process of collaboration is as important as who is doing the work."

"Worrying about the process of how good work happens always stands on the open side of a door. Worrying about credit and immediate reward is a closed door. If you get the right people at the open door, no doors are blocked. That's talent."

Paul thought about this for a moment. He always knew that without the right people he had little chance of success, but he had never internalized the rare nature of talent, how much the stars had to align for talent to be assembled so that people brought out the best in each other.

"I asked you to take me through the process for creating *Ethereal Gaze*," continued Daphne. "You mentioned the pitch, articulation of the concept. I suggested the team came before the concept. How did you go about hiring them?"

"I guess I started the old fashioned way—combing through résumés."

"Of course you immediately recognized the flaw in your approach," offered Daphne. "A résumé only tells part of the story."

"Of course," echoed Paul. "That's exactly what I was thinking."

They both laughed at that. Paul hadn't been thinking that at all. When he'd gotten going on *Ethereal Gaze*, he had been staring at boxes on an organization chart, boxes that had needed to be filled. If those boxes weren't filled, progress would be held back. The open job requisitions had been approved. Stacks of résumés had flowed from human resources to his inbox. Scan, call, interview, interview again, check references, compare notes with others on the interview schedules. It had been his job to put warm bodies in those boxes, right? To get the right people in the right jobs as quickly as possible, with enough time for collaboration and production ahead of the ceaseless deadlines. Hiring was no fun at all. It was a chore. It was a gnawing treadmill. Why did it feel so daunting?

"Hiring is the single most important thing you do as a leader," stated Daphne.

"I suppose firing is the second most important," said Paul.

"Precisely," affirmed Daphne. "Are you familiar with the movie director John Huston, from the classic age of films? *The Maltese Falcon. Treasure of the Sierra Madre. Key Largo. The African Queen.* All of those starred Bogart, each with different co-stars."

"Sort of," said Paul, scribbling the word *Bogart* in his notebook.

🎙 "A résumé only tells part of the story."

Daphne's eyes crossed as she saw him transcribe the wrong name. "Cross out Bogart, write down Huston. As a director, Huston said his most important decisions in filmmaking were around casting. His feeling was, if you got that right, the movie would make itself. His job would consist of saying 'Action,' 'Cut,' and 'Marvelous.' If he got that wrong, he would have to sweat out each scene, each brutally long day under the hot lighting, and that movie still probably wouldn't be any good."

"What about picking the script, like picking the project? Didn't that matter?"

"Of course it did," said Daphne. "But hiring decisions are the most important ones you'll make. Never fill a box. Getting someone onboard is way easier than getting rid of them. As we discussed earlier, the talent you want is in short supply and difficult to assess. Not everyone is as special as they portray themselves to be. You have to bring clarity to the opaque."

"How do you learn to consistently choose wisely?" asked Paul. "How can you ever know for sure? It's hard enough to find someone with the background to do the work."

"Subject matter knowledge is never enough," said Daphne. "When I hire, I look for three things. First is character. Then competency. Then compatibility."

"Not skill set first?" asked Paul. "You just told me that people had to be extraordinary, or aspire to be extraordinary. I look very hard at their credits—what they've done, where they've studied."

"And you should, but line listings in a document they prepared will never tell you if they are honest and if you can trust them. It also doesn't tell you if they believe in teamwork, the sharing of ideas and real collaboration. You may have to start with credentials and bragging rights, but be sure to ask open-ended questions when you interview, thought-provoking questions, not goofy logic questions. Delve into their commitment to learning. Can the person in front of you relearn everything that is changing around them in real time? You're not a journalist collecting facts. You're a dreamer assembling individuals who complement each other."

"What do you look for in their answers?" asked Paul.

"The people you want will reveal that their motivation in getting hired is equally complex. They should have three core needs when they come to you. Do they seek work that is compelling? Do they want to be surrounded by those who bring out the best in them? Do they want to be fairly compensated for what they offer? All three matter equally. Ambition has to be about more than pay. They have to want to share an experience with the other people on your team or you don't get a compounding effect."

"If you focus too heavily on compatibility, doesn't the culture become one of sameness?" asked Paul. "Compatibility sounds so bland."

"Exactly the opposite," said Daphne. "A culture is not meant to be one of sameness. It's meant to reflect multiple points of view. Diversity is how you win."

Paul thought about that for a moment. How could you have both a unified culture and a wide range of viewpoints running simultaneously? Daphne's world view seemed to be part realism, part idealism, part Utopian, and part evangelical. Maybe that's what she meant by aspirational. As he thought about the original release of *Ethereal Gaze*, he saw it met every touch point of those criteria, though when his team had originally come together, they'd never thought about any of that. It had all coalesced naturally.

"When I think about the team we first assembled, I remember how much we argued about things," said Paul. "We argued about every detail. There were so many different points of view to reconcile, but it was important that everyone weighed in with an opinion. It was weird. We argued, but we never fought. It was never personal. It was always about the project, about making it the best we could. You're right. There was so much diversity in the talent and experiences people brought, the culture was a reflection of that, of the wide-ranging opinions. That's a big part of what worked."

"Did you agree on every point and make sure everyone's opinion was incorporated in the final set of decisions?" asked Daphne, speaking slowly and deliberately.

"Not a trick question again?" asked Paul.

Daphne nodded with certainty.

🎤 "Diversity is how you win."

"We'd have to be nuts to include every single opinion," said Paul. "It would have been a mess, a giant set of compromises instead of a unified vision."

"So you as the leader held the vision, you let everyone participate in the raging debate, and each time it was necessary you made the hard calls?" asked Daphne.

"I did," affirmed Paul. "And there was never an uprising, never a revolt. We argued respectfully, and we moved forward when we needed to move forward."

"You discovered that product development is not necessarily democratic," said Daphne. "The process of participation is democratic, reflecting the diversity you assemble in the talent, but there is a rock-hard difference between compromise and consensus."

"Are they really that different?"

"Poison and antidote," described Daphne. "Compromise is a political ploy meant to please the participants in the discussion, not the recipients of the outcome. Compromise does not unify, it dilutes the spectrum of input for the sake of expediency. It alleges to make everyone happy but it makes no one happy. Consensus is momentum building—a tool to test listening and a shared gut-check on progress. Consensus aggregates ideas, then focuses progress on weeding out lesser options for better ones, when guided by a leader who has already established the respect of the team. Consensus has no bias for individual ownership, so no one's feelings get hurt. Team ownership drives the process forward through respect for each other and respect of the leader. No respect, no consensus, nothing visionary will emerge. Respect comes first, and it has to be earned in advance of the process, then earned anew throughout the process."

"I guess I never thought of it that way, but that's how *Ethereal Gaze* happened. We all wanted consensus, but none of us wanted compromise. The final product was able to reflect a point of view, specifically because we had the ability to incorporate more than one point of view in the process at different milestones, without forcing every point of view into every decision."

"Sounds like you made it past department silos and individual egos," said Daphne. "You created a cross-functional team that learned to act as a single unit. No small trick, and the results surpassed what any one of you could do or any one department could do. You created the level playing field with mentorship working in every direction."

"The sequel didn't go that way," continued Paul. "There was so much grandstanding about what to do differently and what to keep the same. People weren't listening to each other. We were too focused on who had the right answer, not what the right answer looked like. I let the debates run on past primetime and we ground to a halt. I didn't maintain a unified vision that was bigger than any one of us."

"Talented people often come with big egos," said Daphne. "Saying something louder doesn't make it right. Listening for a better answer is what makes it right. Bridging the gaps of individual talent requires that acknowledgment, and, in some senses, a bit of finesse and handling."

"Once people get a little success under their belt, it can be a fine line between confidence and hubris," vented Paul.

"Yes, and if they are pleased with limiting their careers to a little success, then they don't have to transform themselves from the accomplished to lifelong learners. If they only want to hear the bell ring once or twice, they're leaving the future to others, which hardly makes them the stars they may think they are. Talent doesn't stand still or look backward, only forward."

Just then Paul's phone rang, as if on cue. He looked at the display screen, immediately recognizing the flashing name.

"This is Randy, my lead software engineer. Would it be impolite if I talked to him for a moment?"

"I'm not one to stand on manners," replied Daphne. "People first. Randy is one of your people."

Paul smiled awkwardly and looked at his handset, but something Daphne had just said stuck in his mind. As he answered his phone, he wondered if he had surrounded himself with individuals amassing credits or a team of lifelong learners. "Randy, hey, what's happening?"

"We got word you were stuck at SFO," said Randy. "Are you going to make it back tonight? Everyone wants to meet tomorrow."

"Saturday Sort-Out?" queried Paul. "We're in between projects. I thought we would take off a few weekends before we got back to full throttle."

"We've got a lot of angst here," explained Randy. "We're hearing rumors the press demos didn't go all that well. The team wants to know what's going on."

"It's not that bad," said Paul. "We need to apply a little polish to the master, like we did with the original. We can still get to where we need to be."

"I'm not so sure," said Randy. "The master is due this week if we're sticking with the production ship date. There's not a lot of time for changes, and I'm not sure we all agree on the changes that need to be made. This crew spends too much time arguing, and it's not the good kind of arguing we used to have."

"I haven't even shared the feedback with you," said Paul. "Why the panic?"

"To tell you the truth, people's phones are ringing," voiced Randy. "Word travels fast in this business. Other studios are already pouncing. Our art director, Helen, keeps saying she's not taking the hit for this, that she just did what we told her to do under protest. She is thinking seriously about taking another gig."

"We can't lose Helen," blurted out Paul. "We need her for the fix. She's amazing. And if this one fails, we need her for the next product. Look, if I make it back, we'll have the Saturday Sort-Out.

Just keep everyone on hold. I'll text you in a few hours and let you know if I'm going to make it. If I don't, you hold the meeting without me."

"I'm not holding the meeting without you," barked Randy. "I hope you make it back and bring everyone together. Things can unravel quickly, you know. You have to bring us together."

"I'll do my best to bring you together," said Paul, and he hung up, attempting to avoid direct eye contact with Daphne.

Daphne had used the break to check a few of her own incoming emails. She had heard Paul's end of the conversation, but not what Randy was saying. Her eyes were already upon Paul.

"Some dissonance on the home front?" asked Daphne. "You need to bring *them* together?"

"Creative people can be touchy. Sometimes the mentorship doesn't flow evenly," said Paul. "They didn't hear from me so I guess they started poking around and heard some of what I heard. I could lose my art director if I don't play this right. She needs a little push."

"Maybe out the door," said Daphne. "How about you need to bring *us* together?"

"I said that wrong, didn't I," erred Paul. "I did say *we* before. I blow that sometimes."

"We all do," confirmed Daphne. "You can't separate you from them—you are them! Look for people who push themselves. Resilience. Self-motivation. You can't force someone to stay committed. It's not your job to be their conscience. For constant improvement to flow naturally, they have to commit and recommit entirely on their own."

🎤 "Look for people who push themselves."

"I'm trying to keep all of this straight," gurgled Paul. "Revere talent. Hire carefully. Encourage diversity. Now you're telling me to get out the boot?"

"I'm telling you people have to want to be on the job for the team to grow," said Daphne. "If someone doesn't want to be there, I'm not sure it matters how much talent they possess. They have to want to give everything they have, and all you can do is create the environment where that's possible. Everything people give is a choice."

Paul wasn't feeling comfortable at all. He was tired. He was edgy. Word of the weak product was leaking. Now his team was in conflict, and he was four hundred miles away waiting for a plane to be fixed or replaced.

"You find it easy to let people go?" asked Paul, more than incredulously.

"Not at all, but I only want to work with people who want to work with me," clarified Daphne. "Try this. Tell me about the worst hire you ever made."

"That's easy," responded Paul. "His name was Darrius, and he was . . . well, I'm not sure I can find the words."

"What did you like about him when you made the offer?"

"Absolutely everything," said Paul. "He was a brilliant composer, a musician who knew every digital sound tool ever created. His work was astonishing, and he had nonstop ideas."

"What was the problem?"

"He wasn't open to feedback of any kind. When someone would offer a comment or suggestion, he would recite how much better he was at his craft than they were at their craft."

"A very defensive fellow. You didn't pick up any of that when you hired him?"

"Not at all," said Paul. "He interviewed perfectly, not just with me, with the entire team. He seemed to have a good sense of humor. Our group likes to laugh and can be a little self-deprecating when things get tense, which is most of the time. That's a big part of our culture. Laughing at ourselves holds us together. It wasn't until after he joined us that he became sarcastic, kind of mean-spirited in the way he deflected roadblocks, and he was never the butt of his own jokes."

"He didn't become that after he filled out his W-4. Obviously he was hiding something when he interviewed. Some people are brilliant at getting in the door. It's a skill they master."

"They have to if they can't make a gig stick," related Paul.

"And when you found out on the job that he wasn't willing to push himself to be a part of the shared mission, it no longer mattered how much he knew about sound recording."

"Exactly—it took a year longer than it should have, but I had to ask him to leave. Then he didn't want to leave and got a lawyer and threatened us. He stopped being funny."

"Was he part of the team on *Ethereal Gaze*?" asked Daphne.

"No, we let him go before that. We promoted his assistant sound designer, and she was a smash. I wish we had figured it out sooner. We wasted so much time, but at least we got it right."

"The creative process can be wild," said Daphne. "Although we make different things, it's not that much different from one industry to the next. The underlying teamwork that allows great work to happen and everyone to contribute their talent is remarkably similar. You establish clear goals and objectives together that everyone understands, then measure everything that can be measured as you go. The paradox emerges when milestones become formulaic and don't reflect sparkle. Innovation is not easy, which is why it is so valuable. When you paint, you make a mess."

"There is always fallout, I'll give you that," said Paul. "Not everyone can take the sparring, round after round. Keeping each other out of the rat holes can be challenging, especially a sharp, hand-picked team who knows what they're doing."

"If they really know what they're doing, they'll understand the delicacy of pruning. True collaboration often requires tearing things down before reinventing them, without tearing each other down. If everyone isn't in it for the same outcome, you may never clean up the muddle."

"My head is starting to spin a little," said Paul. "Maybe it's the wine. Maybe I need some air. My new product is in trouble, my team is freaking out, and my art director may leave. Plus everything

🎤 "When you paint, you make a mess."

you're telling me makes sense, but it's a lot to take in all at once. It's been a weird day."

"That we agree on. I just want you to believe that your repeat success starts with people, and that you have the ability to build great teams by being finicky about the people you bring together. You also need to let creativity happen."

"I try to create the environment you're talking about," said Paul. "Everyone is always so busy. I wish I could find more opportunity to let the team find better answers. The deadlines are brutal. Deadlines are antithetical to creativity. That may have been the problem with our sequel."

"I know, the deadlines can get you every time," agreed Daphne. "They can also get you focused. People can fill their days with unlimited activity. Sometimes they're so busy answering emails they forget that emails aren't the work, they're a tool that lets you do the work. Busy is not always the same thing as productive. You can waste a lot of precious time on people like Darrius, and end up not leaving enough time for the best ideas to emerge."

"Like leaving enough time for the good arguing, the constructive conflict where we don't attack each other," said Paul. "I wonder how many people really understand what creativity is. It's an extremely counterintuitive process, making something come into existence where nothing was before, iterating on a problem until each solution is better than the next. A lot of people think creativity is a magical playground, but it really isn't all that fun. It takes focus, discipline, interminable patience, the willingness to accept failure. How glamorous is that, reworking every module with the clock always ticking?"

"Seems like this point resonates for you," said Daphne. "So if you understand that the process of invention is the process of reinvention, maybe you shouldn't be so worried about whether you lose your art director."

"I think what worries me most is whether my team burned out on this project," said Paul. "After the big hit they were energized, ready to tackle the next one. Now they seem tired."

"I hear you," said Daphne. "If people are burned out at the end of a project, if they have given you all they have to give, then you've delivered a checkpoint, but you've compromised the future. Somehow I'm confident you haven't done that. You need to go back and stir the pot a little, infuse it with new energy, see what happens."

"Can I ask you an awkward question?" said Paul. Daphne nodded. "When we were talking earlier you said something about retiring. What was that all about?"

Daphne tilted her head and looked away a moment, unusually hesitant in finding her words. "Well, in the spirit of candor, I guess I should tell you why I'm actually going to Los Angeles. I seem to have an irregular heartbeat of late. I think it might be genetic, but who knows. It's become a bit more noticeable these last few years; probably an age thing. My regular doctors thought it serious enough that I see a specialist in your hometown. I hope he can steer me in the right direction."

"That's your weekend on the road?" exclaimed Paul. "That's horrible. You haven't said a word about it all night. Are you going to be alright?"

"I'll find out soon enough. I don't like to dwell on it, but I promised my husband I wouldn't brush it off. Tell you what, let me go check on my appointment in case this flight delay is not resolved, and you check to make sure your notebook is up to date. Sound like a plan?"

"A little cavalier for me, but if you don't want me to make a big deal about it, then that's how I'll handle it." Paul didn't know what else to say.

"You're an exceptional listener," said Daphne. "That's solid ground for a leader. Few people in business understand that. People will be accountable to a manager, but they'll only bring forth their full potential when motivated by a leader."

Daphne was an amazing thinker, but in that moment Paul realized she, like everyone else, was not invincible. It made him think even harder about her passion for people first. In that devotion, she was surely resolved. As he looked to his notebook, a few more summary thoughts flowed from his pen.

♩ ♩ ♩

Paul's Notebook: People

♪ ♪ ♪

♪ Seek the extraordinary and revere talent.

♪ Hire for Character, Competency, and Compatibility.

♪ Diversity on your team expands thinking.

♪ Self-demanding beats boss-demanding every time.

♪ Creativity and collaboration require boundless iteration.

Chapter 3: Products

♩ ♩ ♩

When Daphne came back from the service desk, the look on her face told Paul they still weren't going anywhere soon. Paul looked around the room and noticed that every chair was now taken and the noise level was rising. This Friday night at SFO was turning into a marathon wait, but as Daphne had predicted, time was passing quickly with the conversation.

"Now they're saying fog," conveyed Daphne. "The planes at the gate are in working order, but they aren't flying. They haven't cancelled, but that doesn't mean much. Unfortunately, if I cancel I'm going to have to wait another week for my medical appointment, and that doesn't hold much appeal."

"You can't cancel," said Paul. "You need to get to that appointment. If they don't get us on a flight, we can rent a car. I'll drive. I've driven up and down the state dozens of times. You can get a flight back after your appointment or return the car, your choice."

"That's kind of you," said Daphne. "I may take you up on that, but I'll stay optimistic we'll fly at some point tonight."

Paul scoped out the lounge again and took in the frustration around him, all the discontent that everyone was experiencing. He wondered how all the business people there were dealing with their incessant challenges. Were they burned out? Did they have great teams ready to pounce? Had they made their talent choices carefully? Or were they just plodding through their corporate lives, surviving one day to the next, making sure each paycheck found its way into their account, but losing track of the years they lost on tiring political maneuvers? He had seen too many like them already in his career, the road warriors who were always busy, but often not productive enough. Their dreams would slip away, and then one day they would realize what they had traded for those paychecks. That could never be him. One thing they didn't have was a chance meeting with Daphne. He was not going to let one moment of that go to waste.

"I'm not ordering any more to drink, in case we have to drive," said Paul. "I think I've had my fill anyway. You're not really serious about quitting, are you?"

"Like I said, I'll do what makes the most sense. I don't relish the idea of leaving SalientCorp because of a medical concern, but my family has to come first, right there with my health."

"What does your husband do?" asked Paul.

"He teaches computer science at a community college. He is a splendid man. Best career decision I ever made was to marry someone who believes in my dreams as much as I believe in his. We raised two magnificent children together. Our son is a social worker focused on at-risk youth and our daughter designs solar energy panels. All part of an amazing journey I hope you get to enjoy in your future, on top of work success. Want to talk about products?"

"Yes, I want to talk about products," confirmed Paul. "I want to talk about fixing this sequel product that's going to ruin my career. If only I had more time, we could go back and start over."

"It's not going to ruin your career unless you don't play for the comeback," said Daphne. "And you don't have the time to start over, so that's a pipe dream. But what if you did? What would you do differently?"

"Fire Helen the prima donna art director?" suggested Paul.

"You can still do that," said Daphne. "Find out first if she deserves it. Let's talk about the product instead of the people for a moment, even though they are hard to separate. What would Steve Jobs say?"

"Steve Jobs? I have no idea. Beyond my scope. He's beyond reach."

"Don't be so sure," said Daphne. "Everyone who loves innovation studies Steve Jobs. There's a reason. Think about it hard and you'll get it. I just gave you a clue."

"Think Different."

"You got it on the first try," declared Daphne. "That wasn't so hard. What does it mean?"

"It's from his marketing campaign, the one he put in place when he returned to Apple," answered Paul. "It was brilliant, an untouchable campaign."

🎤 "What would Steve Jobs say?"

"Great slogan, huh?" said Daphne.

"The best," agreed Paul. "He relaunched the company on the back of those two words."

"I'm going to take my insignia notebook and pen back from you if that's as far as we've come," rumbled Daphne, a touch impudent. "*Think Different* is not a slogan. It's not even really a marketing tagline. It's a rallying cry."

Another familiar voice from the other side of the bar chimed in: "*Think Different* is practically a religion, even I know that." It was Harold-the-bartender. He was back, this time with a cup of green tea for Daphne. "You're lucky she doesn't give up on you," continued Harold. "Some coffee maybe to wake you up?"

"Yes, thanks," said Paul. He would have said anything to get rid of Harold. He wanted to hear what Daphne had to say next.

"When Steve Jobs returned to Apple, he didn't come back to do the same things he had done before he left. He not only wanted people to rethink computers as naturally connected devices, he wanted to reinvent the music business, mobile phones, even the way we think about portable devices. *Think Different* was his way of declaring war on sameness. It forced his team to challenge themselves to achieve the impossible, and then when they achieved it, make it look simple to everyone else. Only when his team completely embraced that ethos would a product be ready to put in front of customers and clearly exceed their expectations."

"Please, everyone can't create products like Steve Jobs, and I am certainly nowhere close to thinking I'm a Steve Jobs," argued Paul. "I'm more like the people he would rally, just a regular guy who wants to make great things but isn't necessarily sure how to go about it."

"You're right, Steve was special, almost always at the top of his game," agreed Daphne. "Infinitesimally few of us are anything like Steve Jobs, gifted and driven at that level of tackling impossibility. The point is, by aspiring to be extraordinary we can dare ourselves to do the kind of work that Steve Jobs demonstrated. Here's an easy one: Do you consistently remind yourself to Think Different when you approach product development?"

"I'd like to say I do," replied Paul. "I do some of the time, but not all of the time."

"Then do it all the time," asserted Daphne. "You may not get there all the time, but if you don't reach, you'll be stuck in sameness. Incremental ideas don't change markets. That's something we also learned from Steve Jobs. He led by example. We can't create new product categories all the time, but if we understand that category-defining products are what make the big leaps, we know where to set the bar."

"We pulled that off with *Ethereal Gaze*," declared Paul. "It was different, and it was not incremental. It was its own thing."

"All innovation is not created equal," added Daphne. "There's incremental innovation, which

🎤 "Incremental ideas don't change markets."

is fine but not groundbreaking, and there's leap-frogging. With *Ethereal Gaze*, it sounds like you leapfrogged. You didn't take a small step past the competition. You left them in the dust."

"I like the way you say that," said Paul. "Left them in the dust. I don't think we ever intended that. It happened because we brought all the individual elements to bear without thinking about how to one-up anyone."

"This goes back to our discussion of people. You assembled the right team. The people who create leapfrog products eat their own dog food. They don't make products solely for other people. You have to make products you want to use. If you won't use them when you have access to them for free, there's no reason you should expect other people will pay you for the privilege."

"I don't think that's completely fair," said Paul. "There are products people create that they won't have the opportunity to use."

"Yes, I'll give you that. Let's say I was CEO of a company that made baseball gloves, but I couldn't actually play baseball. Could I still eat my own dog food? The answer is yes, because I wouldn't manufacture the gloves if I didn't believe they were outstanding. I would find people around me who played baseball, put the gloves in their hands, and ask them, 'What do you think of these?' Friends, family, strangers playing evening softball in the park, Little Leaguers after school, Minor Leaguers in training camp; heck, if I could get to them, Major Leaguers in stadium dugouts—I would find out *firsthand* if what we were selling was something I could love. Even if I couldn't use them, I would want to love them, and the process by which we made them. I choose that word carefully. You can't just like, you have to love. That's where the creation of a brand begins."

Paul couldn't dispute that, nor did he really want to argue the point. She had connected the dots perfectly. You did have to eat your own dog food to assure the excellence in your product development function, and if you couldn't actually use the products, then you still had to feel strongly enough about their distinction to be a champion of that excellence.

When Harold returned with Paul's coffee, Paul noticed that he'd received a text. With the noise of the room, he hadn't heard the notifying alarm on his mobile. The words on the small screen penetrated his skin: "We're going to get killed on this duck, aren't we?"

He showed the text to Daphne. "Salutations from my boss. His radar is highly tuned."

"That's the problem with the digital age," said Daphne. "Word travels at Internet speed, and you can never be unconnected. What are you going to text him back?"

"I was hoping you might help me wordsmith that," replied Paul. "You've probably been on the receiving end of that kind of thing more than I have. What wouldn't set you off?"

🎤 "You can't just like, you have to love."

"Maybe tell him you didn't reach as far as you could have on this one, but you still can."

Paul thought for a moment how to say that in a text and started typing. Then he stopped. Then he started again. Then he stopped again.

"Simple, honest, to the point," directed Daphne.

Paul typed the words: "We should have loved it more . . . I'm on it." Then he hit send.

"Remember when you asked me if my boss was a good guy? I think we're about to find out. Maybe we won't need to rent that car after all."

"He was smart enough to hire you. He's not going to fire you for being honest. He must know talent. If he doesn't, that's his loss. The experience you gained with that sequel is priceless. You know what not to do again. You learned the hard way, and you own it. If you don't love it, why should your customers?"

"You have to eat your own dog food," repeated Paul. "If you don't, why should they? Think Different, aim to leapfrog, love not like. What else?"

"It's not enough to love your product. You have to love your customers, too, every single one—those who complain the most are the ones who control the keys to your survival. Customers now have vast, often unlimited choices. That's a big part of what's different today."

"It was easier when you were coming up through the ranks like me, wasn't it?" asked Paul.

"In some ways," said Daphne. "We didn't have all the tools that connect us, but we had some constraints on distribution that don't exist anymore. If I could learn to evolve with increased competition and speed to market, so can you."

Paul's phone dinged. It was the text alarm. He was afraid to look, but he knew the Band-Aid had to be ripped off in one pull. He turned over the handset so they could both see it at the same time. The text read: "We'll talk when you get back."

"I'm not off the hook," grumbled Paul. "Not even a little."

"Did you expect you would be with a simple text?" asked Daphne. "He's your boss, not your father. How much did your company invest in the sequel?"

"Millions. We're not going to lose all of it. We may not lose any of it. We just aren't going to make the kind of money we made on the original. Sequels in my business are supposed to do better than the originals as the brand and market expand. Everything we do can't be a winner."

"Would you let Randy or Helen off the hot seat for mediocre performance with just a text?"

"No, of course not," said Paul. "I would remind them that there is no growth without risk, that we have to be willing to try things and fail, but when we fail we have to learn. It's not failure if it's learning, but there has to be learning. You have to capture that learning and harness it."

"I suppose he'll say something to the same effect," said Daphne. "Of course, I've never met

🎤 "Customers now have vast, often unlimited choices."

him, so you never know. He could mop the floor with you to make him feel better."

"Thanks, I feel so much more chipper," grimaced Paul.

"You should," said Daphne. "Think about the opposite spectrum. Suppose you weren't willing to risk failure and learn. Suppose you devoted all your energy to protecting the status quo. Think of a company that isn't around anymore that tried that trick."

"Kodak comes to mind," said Paul. "I read somewhere that they developed the first digital camera in 1975, but kept it off the market because they were afraid of what it might do to their traditional film processing business."

"Polaroid missed the shift to digital as well," replied Daphne. "They didn't have to stick with mechanical, self-developing prints. That was a choice."

"It's amazing how bad the blunders can be," continued Paul. "Borders Books, Circuit City, Tower Records—they're gone forever. With all the customers they had, the vast resources, all that talent and cash in the bank, these days they're just names, empty shells. Businesses become nostalgia."

"Tombstones, actually, all in the Dead Brand Graveyard," said Daphne. "No Endless Encores there. The list goes on and on: Palm, Zenith, Blockbuster, CompUSA, Wang Laboratories—all once beloved brands, all now decaying tales of yesteryear. Now think of the once great brands about to fail, the ones you know will soon evaporate. What is their idea of risk?"

"Way too conservative," answered Paul. "They're afraid to take risks because they're afraid of failing, when in fact they're already failing by refusing to dance a little closer to the edge."

"Compare that to companies like IBM or General Electric, that have been reinventing themselves for over a hundred years. IBM used to sell mainframe hardware, punch cards, and Selectric typewriters. Today it's focused on consulting services, system design, and artificial intelligence like Watson. GE was born from the vision of Thomas Edison selling indoor lighting, then later *modern* appliances like toaster ovens and clock radios. It was reinvented under Jack Welch to sell advanced medical equipment, aircraft engines, and financial services."

"I get it," said Paul. "Those iconic companies only lasted because they didn't stay the same. They are the exception, not the norm."

"No industry is spared if it fails to reinvent itself," continued Daphne. "If you don't shake it up, creative destruction eats your lunch. You risk, you test, you learn, you live another day. The alternative is way worse than a tidy failure."

"There's no clear path to longevity," sighed Paul. "You risk losing what you already have in order to win a longer game, or you can lose everything there is to lose, including the chance to try again. Was it really a lot easier when there were more constraints on distribution, when customers had fewer choices and you could find a way to sell a product like our sequel with less competition?"

"Not entirely. Too often we flew blind without enough connection to our customers," admitted Daphne. "The main difference is that the boss used to be the individual responsible for your performance, like the gentleman who sent you that text, someone higher up the organization chart. With constraints on distribution removed in a fast moving global economy, your real boss is your customer. You and your organization chart boss actually have the same real boss, and he knows that. That's why he is concerned about the product and its success, not simply because of the millions already invested and the opportunity cost, but for the loyalty it will or won't build for you. Every shot you take with your customers has to set up the next shot. Just because they are with you today doesn't mean they will be tomorrow. Loyalty has to be won and re-won at every touch point."

"And that's why every product has to be exceptional," summarized Paul. "Every product has to matter, or you lose them."

"Your boss always has the choice to leave you," said Daphne. "They fire you by abandoning you. It's not as obvious as your office boss giving you your walking papers, but it's just as painful, and just as hard to rebound from. Maybe harder. *Good enough* has nothing to do with good. *Good enough* is the straight shot to mediocrity."

"It's a daunting challenge to keep customers coming back, to beat back creative destruction over and over again. Why would anyone even try?" suggested Paul. "Think Different, leapfrog, love, compete without distribution advantage—where does it end?"

"It doesn't, yet people still manage to win. Many times the same people," said Daphne. "That's what you said you wanted—to be a repeat winner, to have a limitless string of product success, not be a one-hit wonder."

"Like those bands we talked about earlier—the ones who repeat, the ones who don't. Ray Charles vs. the Bay City Rollers."

"The remarkable is hard to question," added Daphne. "Not long ago I was at a Paul McCartney concert. He played for three hours in front of fifty thousand people, played thirty-nine songs, sang every one. He had the crowd in the palm of his hand the entire show."

"Somehow I don't have a hard time seeing you there," said Paul.

"I'll take that as a compliment," replied Daphne. "You know what landed the clearest for me at that thundering rock show?"

"The sheer number of hits from every phase of his career?"

"The sheer bravery of introducing four new songs the crowd hadn't heard before," avowed Daphne. "Yes, he gave them the hits they wanted— from the Beatles, from Wings, from his solo career. Yet he had the courage to bring new material forward, not knowing if they'd like it, knowing they'd

probably prefer another hit. He made sure 10% of
the show was unfamiliar to his fans, people who
had paid big money to hear his hits. Even in his
seventies, he dared to reinvent himself in front
of a giant crowd, risking the moment, willing to
be rejected, still knowing that there can never be
a new hit until you debut it. He didn't need to do
that, not Paul McCartney, but he did it anyway. The
creativity could never run dormant in him. He had
to satisfy as well as introduce. That's a star."

"Great, now I have to be Steve Jobs *and* Paul
McCartney to survive," quipped Paul.

"You have to be *like* Steve Jobs and Paul
McCartney, learn from their example," contended
Daphne. "You see, there's a secret that's lurking in
the shadows that makes it all possible."

"The guys who get Endless Encores are god-
like?"

"Not at all, but they do know this: The world
is filled with 90-percenters. Once you know that
secret, you know the bar you need to get over."

"For those of us who aren't Jobs or McCartney,
what's so bad about getting to 90%?" asked Paul.
"Ninety percent is pretty darn good. In school, 90%
is an A-minus. You can have a 4.0 grade point aver-
age if every grade you get is an A-minus."

"If only that were the case in business," laughed
Daphne. "In business, an A-minus is all you need
to lose a customer forever. Remember, your customer has choices. If your customers can have
an A or even an A-plus, why would they pay their
hard earned dollars for an A-minus? GPA may be
a level playing field on your scholastic record, but

🎤 "The world is filled with 90-percenters."

don't even try to hide behind averages when you're asking someone for their repeat business and customer loyalty."

"Now you're telling me that to win the product development game our team has to deliver a perfect A or better all the time? Daunting just became unreachable."

"I'm telling you that almost everyone out there who wants to get to 90% probably can find a way there, so if you want to win in an arena without constraints on distribution, you have to be better than that. You have to set your bar that high, and challenge your team to get over it. There is zero chance that you will do it every time. It is a lofty goal, a pure ideal, and fully unattainable. Touch that bar more often than your competitors, make the statement that you are always looking to be there with your customers, and your GPA will come in higher than 4.0. You make better products by expecting better products, by demanding better products of yourself and your team, the kind of products that make it clear to your big boss that you care. That's walking the walk. That's how you demonstrate in real time that you have learned to Think Different."

"Is this the stump speech for quality assurance?" asked Paul.

"Depends on what you mean by quality," replied Daphne. "In software development, a lot of companies think of quality assurance as the last step in the process, as a gate the product has to go through before it is released to customers, to get a stamp that it is defect-free. Is that how you work when you develop videogames?"

"I hate to admit it, but I'm afraid so," revealed Paul.

"Don't feel alone. A lot of companies work that way," said Daphne. "Medical device companies, pharmaceuticals, food manufacturers—many of them have their R&D function entirely separate from their quality assurance departments, which give a thumbs-up, thumbs-down decision as the last phase in the development cycle. In my experience, that's cynical. I think quality assurance is a process, not a department. If you want A-plus products on a regular basis, you need the process of *assuring quality* at every stage of product development, from concept to delivery. That's how you consistently distinguish yourself from your competition."

"The boss notices that kind of quality, huh?"

"We do, as customers, in every choice we make, because the choice is ours."

"I've been taking a lot of notes, but I'm still going to have trouble explaining this to my day-to-day boss," said Paul. "The guy who hired me. The guy who texted me. The guy who wants to discuss it when I get back."

"Hopefully you will get back in time for that Saturday Sort-Out. Your team can help you find the answers."

"And hopefully your heart will keep beating strong for a long time," said Paul. "There's no way you can walk off the job. You know too much."

"You've got me thinking about that," responded Daphne. "Talking with you this evening has started to fire me up a bit. We still have one topic to go, though, if you're not exhausted."

"I am exhausted," said Paul. "I'm sure you are as well. I just hope they don't call our flight and you leave me with a cliffhanger."

"I'll talk faster," said Daphne. "This next part is really quite simple."

Paul looked out the window toward the tarmac and couldn't see much. The dense fog was everywhere in full ghostly form, a San Francisco night out of the movies. He looked up at the flight board and almost every listing was still marked "Delayed." One way or another Daphne would get to her appointment, he would see to that, but first he would get the next chapter. For that he was quietly grateful.

♩ ♩ ♩

Paul's Notebook: Products

♫ ♫ ♫

♪ Think Different is not a slogan.

♪ Leapfrog products invent and reinvent markets.

♪ Eat your own dog food.

♪ Don't confuse "good enough" with good.

♪ Quality assurance is a process, not a department.

Chapter 4: Profits

♪ ♪ ♪

The din in the lounge was becoming overwhelming. The clock was nearing midnight and many flights were being cancelled, especially into smaller airports where flights wouldn't be allowed to land this late. Waiting passengers were angry, chewing out staff at the service desk, as if somehow the fog and equipment delays were their fault. Daphne and Paul had to talk louder over the noise to hear each other, at times bordering on shouting. It was a bit comical to be bellowing at each other in public given the topics at hand, yet weirdly comfortable with the rapport they had established.

"I wonder if people realize how stupid they sound when they yell at other people who can help them and aren't to blame for the mishap they want corrected," suggested Paul.

"No, they forget to think about being on the other side of the desk when they are on this side of the desk," replied Daphne. "It makes no sense that people forfeit their humility for their selfishness, but they do. Being a good customer is another great learning opportunity."

"I'm guessing around midnight they are going to shut this place down and cancel the rest of the flights," said Paul. "Still up for the drive?"

"No, I'm pretty tired," said Daphne. "I'm a little too old for all-nighters; plus it might not be great for my heart."

"Then quickly, tell me about profits," begged Paul. "This is the good part, right? Teach me how to bring home the big bucks in ways I can't imagine—after, of course, I've hired extraordinary people and built extraordinary products."

"It's not much of a mystery," offered Daphne. "Math is not magic. The numbers are what the numbers are."

"You don't expect me to bite on that," said Paul.

"Bite on what you want," volleyed Daphne. "You give me an electronic spreadsheet, I can make it spit out any totals you like. I can put in simple or complex formulas. I can forecast revenue and expenses with uplifting optimism or debilitating pessimism. Fancy a hockey stick going in any direction? We can graph that concoction in red or black. In the end, I can't read the future any better than you can. When it's not the future anymore, for all mortals hindsight is a perfect twenty-twenty. Thus my advice to maintain credibility and stay out of jail: Be authentic in how you forecast; be honest in what you report."

"So don't guess and don't lie?" asked Paul. "Come on, you've got more than that."

"How about build a business model that's sensible, and test your assumptions as often as you

🎤 "The numbers are what the numbers are."

can with accurate data from as many inputs as you can collect."

"Better, but what's a sensible business model?"

"One that's not built from a house of cards because it's what your investors think they want to hear to justify a lunatic valuation. There are speculators who think that way, but if you try to please them with a solve-to mentality, you'll drive yourself to insanity."

"Or to drink?"

"You will crash and burn. Sooner or later, the thin ice shatters, the house of cards folds into the velvet. Build your balance sheet on a sound foundation. The numbers have to work. It's foolish to pretend otherwise."

"What about the stories you hear about companies that were created without a business model, with magnificent technology developed outside the constraints of a business model? Google comes to mind."

"There are always outliers, but remember this: Google has its public valuation today because it has one of the smartest business models ever, a sound balance sheet, enormous free cash flow, a lot of top talent, and world class products. Certainly on an experimental R&D phase you can start on a project without a business model, but you better find one where the numbers add up eventually or you're sunk. No hocus pocus. If you want repeat success, you better have a bulletproof business model, you better understand how it works end to end, and it better not have measurable terminal value out of the gate. Building free cash flow gives you the flexibility to try new R&D projects outside of everyday pressure and off the clock. You can't burn cash forever and expect that someone else will pay your bills."

"It's a little ridiculous that we're talking about this," said Paul. "I mean, before the digital age, before the new millennium, could it have been possible for piled up waves of companies with unproven or untested business models to fly?"

"Depends on who is setting the agenda," answered Daphne. "Is it the gamblers betting the full spread of opportunities they can unearth, playing a numbers game where winners pay for losers, or is it the operators seeking to change the world?"

"Daphne, you know that dreamers can get you in a heap of trouble. Wild thinkers have burned just as much cash as backroom betting shops working the odds."

"There have always been long-range visionaries in business," said Daphne. "Henry Ford, Walt Disney, Bill Gates—people who changed the world through unconventional logic, perhaps not necessarily thinking first about making money. Remember, we don't want to think about profits first, but we do want to be sure someone is thinking about them at some point, when investors and stakeholders expect them. The best of these entrepreneurs surrounded themselves with reliable, straightforward colleagues, who filled out their skill sets and told them the truth. Hype makes for bad decisions."

"Tell me about it! I wasn't even sure I wanted to do the sequel to *Ethereal Gaze*, but when a bunch of top management cornered me with a spreadsheet and showed me how much money we could make if the follow-on product captured the 'slam dunk' market share they thought it would, I smiled and got on board. They were all about profits, but in the wrong order."

"Isn't it strange how groupthink so often masks itself in a company as strategy?" asked Daphne. "Strategy is putting all the chess pieces on the board and imagining what might happen in any number of scenarios. Setting a strategic course might begin with boiling the ocean for possibilities, but if you force the answer you want to hear in advance of vetting an open debate, you're making a move, not envisioning the possible as well as the problematic."

"That's how fads bulldoze the human mind, isn't it?" suggested Paul. "Possibility is not probability. You need more than a small chunk of a large segment to get to a breakthrough."

"Certainly, you can't let a potential hole in the market dictate your commitment, but you also don't have to be fearful of fads," replied Daphne. "In many ways, most of what business produces is a fad. We will drive cars for a long time, but probably not forever. We've been playing physical media forms of music and video for a long time, but that's coming to an end. Your current videogame may only last a month or a year, but people have been playing games for thousands of years. The point of a fad as it pertains to business is more about understanding

🎤 "Hype makes for bad decisions."

how long the fad might last, and investing commensurate with the product lifespan."

"So the mistake is not to ride the wave. The mistake is to assume that the wave will last longer than it will take to get your bait back?" asked Paul.

"Every success has a window of opportunity. Windows can be long or short—either can be profitable if you invest accordingly. You get into trouble when you purposely misunderstand or grossly misjudge the size of the window. That's when hype gets you. That's when strategy becomes a document in a binder shelved on the wall that everyone forgot as soon as the appendices were printed."

"Seems to me that investment and strategy go hand in hand. They're inseparable," added Paul. "You figure out what pieces you have, and what you need to round out the matrix before you act, not after you've already jumped off the cliff."

"You're going to keep tuning along the way," said Daphne. "The point is that speculating and investing are not the same. They overlap like intersecting sine curves, but investing is about creating something built for the long haul, layer upon layer to which you can add, depending on how circumstances unfold. Market forces are always well beyond your control, but a business designed for long-term investment will be flexible enough to absorb the impact of the unknown."

"Focus on what you can control and roll with the punches on what you can't?"

"Exactly. You have to leave room in your action plan to ride the ebb and flow of aggressive competition, political changes, government policy, natural disasters, and, of course, the input of customers," conveyed Daphne. "Speculating is going with a hunch, betting on crystal ball predictions, and praying that your prescribed notion of an outcome will be in actuality what you ordained. Crazy bets do come in, but they are just that, gambles—not investments, and not strategy."

There was a modest rumble in the room. A flight had been called. It was not Daphne and Paul's flight to Los Angeles, but both were heartened by the rustling of computer bags and rollaboards around them as fellow passengers-in-waiting began ambling to the door. It had been a long night, but now it appeared the delay would not go on forever, nor the conversation.

"We have hope," proclaimed Paul. "We're going to get out of here."

"Hope is the strength that keeps us going," said Daphne, watching people around her happily begin to leave the airport lounge. Since their flight wasn't leaving, she had no reason to follow them, but she knew her remaining time with Paul would be limited.

"When you set out to determine strategy, how do you think about building the business so it keeps growing?" continued Paul. "No sane executive wants to lead a company into the Dead Brand Graveyard, yet so many end up there. Suppose they have the best people and the best products. How do they get their head around a business model that is going to both work now and expand into the future?"

"That's the greatest enigma of all," answered Daphne. "You have to think about recurring revenue alongside new revenue. Some transactions have to be there without your prodding, so you can add new transactions on top of them. If you're going to spend money to acquire new customers, you have to balance that with what you're spending to retain the ones you have. If all you do is spend to acquire new business, your margins will be perpetually squeezed. No fun, I assure you."

"My boss says that all the time," agreed Paul. "If every year you start the P&L from zero, it's virtually impossible to grow. You have to know there is some business already on its way from your catalogue of products, and on top of that you add new product introductions."

"Smart guy, your boss," said Daphne. "He gets the mix a lot of us miss. Maybe he was at the same Paul McCartney concert I attended."

"The same boss who isn't going to can me for this lackluster sequel?"

"Yes, that clever fellow. Let me ask you something about that catalogue of products, the base of recurring revenue. Do you cannibalize your own markets before the competition does it for you?"

"Well, we don't put out the same videogames, so it's not exactly possible," said Paul. "But if you're asking do we sometimes leave one out there longer than we should to extract the last bit of profit from it, yeah, we do that sometimes."

"How does it make you feel?"

"Queasy"

"Me, too," winced Daphne. "I think we all do it to some extent, but the key to all of this is balance. Yes, you need a base of recurring revenue, but if you don't give your customers something new and exciting before your competitors do, they will sweep your customers into their camp. You have to study and manage the ratios of evergreen and introductory endeavors at work in all your sales channels. Remember, constraints on distribution are low, choices are high."

"It's staggeringly hard to find the stamina to pull a product from the shelf when it's still selling," said Paul. "R&D costs are ridiculously high. We need all the sales we can muster for contribution margin to make sense."

"One of the hardest choices in business is to pull a product while it's still moving. Again, what we are talking about is strategy. Of course you don't want to leave more money on the table than you should, but you'll often find you need to leave some. If you don't do it, your competitors will happily obviate your offerings. That can be the end of one brand and the birth of a new one that is no longer yours."

"Competitors certainly don't have a moral problem with making you look stupid for holding onto antiquities," echoed Paul. "You're right—it's one of the most difficult choices we have to make."

"If what you do isn't difficult, don't expect to hang around long," said Daphne. "That's what makes our jobs exciting. We have to find some form of turf that's defensible, any form of virtual moat.

🎤 "Do you cannibalize your own markets before the competition does it for you?"

Even commodities can enjoy loyalty if customers form a relationship with a preferred provider. You must bring your customers back to you somehow, some way, to buy what you have been offering, and then sample what you newly offer. That's showing respect for their hard earned dollars."

"I wish when I was a customer people thought of me with that kind of respect," said Paul. "I buy tons of junk I don't like."

"How many times?" asked Daphne.

"Good point. I'm not very forgiving when a company takes me for granted."

"Nor should you be," said Daphne. "We're all customers. We all have choices. Being a good customer means sharing constructive feedback when a company wants to listen, but not giving them your repeat business if they haven't earned it."

Paul looked around the room and saw people leaving. He looked at the listing board and saw the LA flight was still pending, but he knew he was running out of time. He still had so many questions. He also took note of a run-down guy around the edge of the bar who seemed to be listening closely to their conversation. He appeared to be younger than Daphne, but not much.

"How do your financial backers plug into the equation?" inquired Paul. "Your investors, your bankers, even your CFO? How do you keep all those relationships and responsibilities rolling along smoothly when you're consumed with people excellence, product excellence, business model and strategic planning excellence? It almost seems tactical, a big bucket of impossible money metrics and statistical details demanding constant attention."

"I'm old fashioned, but I always treat other people's money like it was my own," said Daphne. "Access to capital is a privilege. A customer's satisfaction and trust are everything to your success, but right there with the customer relationship is how you handle debt and equity."

"Isn't that covered by the risk profile of the investor?" suggested Paul. "It's kind of up to them to pick and choose where they place money wisely."

"It's kind of up to you to give them a reason to trust, and provide them with ongoing reason to continue to trust. In my mind, you don't have a choice."

"Cash is not the easiest thing in the world to manage when you're consumed with creativity and customer satisfaction," said Paul. Then he paused, as if he wished he could take that back. Instead he corrected himself. "I know, if it weren't hard, they wouldn't pay me much to do it."

"You do listen," said Daphne. "I like that about you. I also hope you understand that every spending decision is a reinforcement of your values. What you do, your team will emulate. If you spend uncontrollably, your team will spend the same way. If you bid out every subcontract competitively, your team will know that matters to you. Your actions are far more important than your words. When it comes

🎤 "Access to capital is a privilege."

to your wallet, your actions must be consistent with what you say."

"You and my boss are so similar in a lot of ways," said Paul. "Be frugal, not cheap. He says that all the time."

"Your boss and I probably had a lot of the same bumps on the head. It hurts getting thrown down the elevator shaft for an unnecessary gaffe in judgment. With financial management, the more you're seen using cash wisely, the more you'll have at ready availability. Trust matters. Credit matters, too. We may tally our business reporting using accrual methodology, but we pay our bills using cash. You always need more than you think, so when you spend it, do it as if you are convinced you are always being watched by someone more frugal than yourself, with more cash under their management than you can conceive. Responsibility does scale."

"You won't see me flying first class tonight," noted Paul.

"I'm sorry to hear that," laughed Daphne. "I will be. Of course, I'm not paying for it. I'm just a good customer whom they like to upgrade. It's a backhanded kind of reward, but I'll take it."

"Of course," chuckled Paul. "You've obviously earned it, knowing how to be a good customer."

The stranger around the edge of the bar wasn't laughing with them. Perhaps Paul was imagining it, but he seemed to be peering harder at them.

Paul was starting to become uncomfortable, but with the room beginning to thin, he was able to lower his voice a little.

"You should think about teaching a class in this stuff," said Paul. "You know a lot, and you have a way of sharing it that isn't threatening."

"I'm not sure my team would always agree with you on that," said Daphne. "It's always easier to trade ideas away from the office, and tremendously easier one on one. There's one last thing I would like you to think about when you're building that game-changing business model."

"And that is?"

"Price. It really matters, particularly in an age of unlimited choice. Price is where the rubber hits the road, and it is one of the hardest things to master."

"What makes pricing such a challenge?" asked Paul. "You charge as much as you can, and stay wary of your place in the competitive landscape."

"I wish it were that easy. Price is an abstract. No single price point is ever perfect."

"Right, so you raise prices when you can, and you lower them when you have to. Doesn't seem that complicated to me."

"Price is massively complicated," asserted Daphne. "You need to protect margins, you need to be competitive, you need to feed the business model for today and tomorrow, you need to keep trust in play with your customers. If anyone claimed that pricing strategy was a cake walk, I'd fire them."

"That's awfully harsh," said Paul.

𝕌 "No single price point is ever perfect."

"Price matters that much," responded Daphne. "In today's global economy, price is almost always transparent. Your customers can shop and compare in real time, usually from a mobile device in their hand. I'm not just talking about standing in a store showrooming everyday consumer products. I'm talking factories, leases, raw materials, even the cost of capital. To doubt or misunderstand elasticity is to put your business at constant risk."

"Elasticity, as in, volume goes up as price goes down, and sales go down as price goes up?"

"Precisely. You can deliver improved profits either way—increasing margin while lowering volume, or lowering margin while increasing volume—or any combination of variances. There are infinite nuances you can apply, but you have to be testing your assumptions all the time. By testing, I don't mean guessing. I mean observing variations against a control with quantifiable rigor and then interpreting behavioral impact. Collect and study all the data that's available to you. Optimizing price is now more science than art. You can't leave it to chance. Ignore data at your own peril. Learning to read data is how you assess what resonates with your customers and where you're missing the mark."

"I see your point," said Paul. "Customers can be fickle. Leave too much money on the table, and you aren't treating cash like it's your own. Leave none on the table, and your customers look elsewhere for a deal. It even happens in videogames, where we have a unique product. If we know we have a hit and our price is too high, customers can buy a different game. If we try to become number one by selling at deep discount, we may not recoup our investment no matter how many units we sell."

"Presuming your product delivers the quality levels we discussed, if you sell 100% of your inventory in an instant, you probably priced it too low. If you find yourself with a huge oversupply, you probably priced it too high. Always look for a near sell-out to know you priced optimally, with just enough left unsold to let you know you didn't miss any opportunity and treated your customers fairly."

"Getting to a near sell-out requires pretty astute analysis," said Paul.

"As I said, price is no small trick, and you can't forget about understanding your costs when you set prices. It's not your customer's problem to know what something costs you to create, but it does not live in a vacuum. Manufacturing efficiency can be key to your pricing strategy."

"Again, you and my boss have so much in common," replied Paul. "I used to only focus on R&D costs, the cost to deliver the golden master, or first article. Of course we recoup a small part of that on each unit we sell, but it wasn't until I started paying close attention to the cost to deliver every subsequent unit that I really came to understand what goes into profitability."

"If your manufacturing function is designed with repeatable efficiency, your production model

will be defensible. Your customers enjoy your benefit. Behold the win-win!"

It was at that moment that the sadly intoxi-
cated individual a few seats away from them at the
bar inserted himself into their conversation. A few
hours ago he might have been a distinguished executive in a meeting somewhere making a pitch, but
at the moment he smelled of vodka and grapefruit
juice. He could no longer hold back his opinions.

"You know, I've been listening to your babble
for the last hour or so, and most of it I could let
slide, but this last bit about profits coming after
everything else is nonsense."

"Where do you think profits fit in the equation?" asked Daphne politely.

"You start with profits, you end with profits,"
professed the intruder. "End of argument."

"So you think we have it all wrong, that
we're babbling senselessly?" chided Daphne, now
uncharacteristically antagonistic. "Tell me, what's
your name?"

"Felix," said the stranger. "Felix the cat. The
wonderful, wonderful cat. Why would I tell you my
name?"

"Why would you stick your nose in our conversation?" asked Paul. "If you want to participate,
show some collegiality. You've probably been drinking too much to do that."

"I've been drinking, mostly to drown out your
noise," rejoined Felix. "Let me tell you this, Luke
Skywalker. Obi Wan tells a fine story, but Yoda
keeps the checkbook. You make money for your
boss, you'll do well. You worry about arts and crafts,

you'll be an arts and crafts dude, living in a tie-dyed tent in Golden Gate Park."

"Felix, what do you do for a living?" asked Daphne.

"I'm an institutional investor," announced Felix. "I run a growth and income fund. I look at data, like you told him to do, but I don't let it confuse me and I don't get distracted by long-winded theories. You show me you can make money, I'll take a position. That's what matters."

"You're obsessed with performance," said Daphne. "You're all about report cards. How a business actually creates value can remain opaque. You don't see that as narrow?"

"Idealism is joyously entertaining for bar chat," said Felix. "It's not how most companies operate. Think about all the companies around you—travel, utilities, construction, manufacturing, finance, insurance—what do they put first? In any decent board room, the bottom line is the whole shooting match. You may be the exception, Madam CEO, and I applaud you for your principles, but give this kid a reality check or you're going to nuke his future before he has one."

"So because a lot of businesses do it wrong, that makes it the model path?" challenged Daphne. "You think Paul should run his business the way you measure excellence?"

"Numbers game. I win more than I lose," said Felix, smothering a slight belch. "Life's been good. To me. So far."

Paul looked silently to Daphne to see where she would take the affront. She was undeterred and didn't miss a beat.

"Then if that works for you, keep doing it," offered Daphne. "What works for me, works for me. Paul will figure out what works for him."

"I wish I had more time to debunk your crapola," snarled Felix. "Lucky for you, the board is flashing. All the flights have been called. I'll be leaving now."

"May your winning streak continue indefinitely," bid Daphne. "And that is heartfelt."

Felix departed with her valediction, though not exactly in a straight path. It was an unsettling moment, and suddenly Paul felt much less inspired, much closer to earth. The reality of his lackluster sequel rushed back into his mind. He had to meet with Randy and the team, figure out what do about Helen, talk to his boss. Somehow he had to survive this product cycle for the chance to try again. The LA flight listing had gone green, no longer pending, boarding now, as if responding to a cue.

"Any chance Felix has a point?" asked Paul sheepishly.

"Of course he does. To his credit, he may be right about who's in the majority. You have a bigger question to ask yourself. What do you want your life to be about, and how do your values align with your ambition? Like I said, that's very personal. You have to decide how you can be consistent."

"He seems like an unhappy man, though likely a wealthy one. I wonder what kind of music he likes."

"At least he's honest, Paul. He's telling you what he thinks. He believes every word of that as deeply as I believe what I do. You're going to have to deal with people like him. He may own shares in your company. Guys like Felix are a reality. How you protect your values and keep him happy—or at least at a safe distance—will in many ways ultimately define your success."

Paul shrugged, trying to refocus. "He's right about one thing. The flights are departing. We're almost out of time. What's left?"

"Just your promise," said Daphne. "Let's walk to the gate."

As they were leaving, Harold-the-bartender shouted out to Paul, "Don't mind the nasty drunk. I'll give you two hundred bucks for that notebook."

"Not a chance," said Paul. "Not a chance."

♫ ♫ ♫

Paul's Notebook: Profits
♩ ♩ ♩

♪ A business model is not an afterthought.

♪ Strategy is charting a course, not making a move.

♪ Recurring revenue is the foundation for growth.

♪ Use cash wisely, as if it were out of your own pocket.

♪ Price always matters.

Chapter 5: Departing

♪ ♪ ♪

Despite the late hour, there was new energy emanating throughout the airport as Daphne and Paul exited the lounge and made their way through the concourse. Smiles were to be seen as lines formed to board departing flights. As Daphne and Paul approached their gate, Daphne unexpectedly turned to him and said, "I forgot to ask you: What do you think a brand is?"

"Oh, one more thing, like Steve Jobs would say?" joked Paul. "I'm not sure I have a brilliant answer for you. Why, in the context of Endless Encores, does that matter?"

"You asked me when we started how to protect your career from being a one-hit wonder," explained Daphne. "The key to that is developing a brand."

"Isn't the whole brand thing what got me into this sludge?" asked Paul. "I mean, I had a giant winner, then I made another one sort of like the first, but not different enough to light up people's imaginations. We applied the same name and logo. No one is excited about it."

"A brand is not a name and logo," countered Daphne. "What you did is called a *brand slap*. You leveraged the goodwill you had established in *Ethereal Gaze* and stuck it on the packaging and sell sheet. That can be a predictable enough way to generate a little short-term cash, but it has little to do with building a brand."

"Business people blather on about branding *ad nauseam*," commented Paul. "Everyone has an opinion of what a brand is. It's such an overused term, it hardly means anything anymore. There are so many clichés out there about this brand, that brand, my brand, your brand. How would you define a brand?"

"A brand is a promise."

"A promise of what?" reacted Paul.

"Exactly correct," added Daphne. "That's our job, to define the promise. I assure you, when a brand is handled properly, practically with kid gloves, it can mean a great deal, the bond that endures and rejuvenates. It can elevate you to soaring new heights, or sink you deep like a steel link chain fixed to the ocean floor."

"I'm not sure I get it," exhaled Paul. "Walmart is a promise? The *New York Times* is a promise? Apple is a promise? That's how they stay off the ocean floor?"

"Yes, absolutely. Walmart, in their customers' minds, means best everyday low prices, period—no worries about deep discount promotions that come and go. The *New York Times* means *The Paper of Record*, getting the facts right, sharing the news in real time and archiving history. Apple means humanity before technology, no manual required. Those are promises, simple but profound, said or

🎙 "A brand is a promise."

unsaid. They are rallying cries within their companies and among their stakeholders, not the least
of which are customers. They are mission-critical
touch points, benchmarks of reference anytime
the landscape becomes hazy. Most importantly, to
grow and continue building on success, they are
promises these companies must keep or risk losing
everything."

"When you say it that succinctly, it sounds like
we created an expectation with the original *Ethereal Gaze*, and then didn't meet that expectation
with the sequel," observed Paul.

Daphne set down her shoulder bag as they
reached the boarding area. "That can be the challenge with a brand promise. Once you make a
promise, people expect you to keep that promise
anytime you reference it. Once you have a brand
in the market, it's yours to protect, and yours to
lose. Brand building is a continuum that everyone
in your company owns jointly—from ideation to
customer engagement. Believing it is somehow a
marketing ploy is the surest tunnel to collapse."

"We think the hardest thing in the world is to
put a brand on the map," said Paul. "It's harder to
keep it on the map."

"It's even harder to expand it. If you take advantage of brand equity and try to unduly harvest
value from the goodwill you've established with
your customers, the recourse can be severe. It's the
right problem to have, worrying if your next brand

extension lives up to the promise you've already defined. In your case, *Ethereal Gaze 2* is not a bad product; it's just not as exciting and imaginative as the original. On its own it might have been fine; maybe not a megahit, but when people compare it to the original, they have a frame of reference for the excellence they expect."

"We set our own bar too high."

"Indeed, and now you have to get over it or it's a letdown. By the way, Paul, I don't think it's too late to polish it a little. My sense is that wouldn't be throwing good money after bad. It would be doubling down on a core asset. That's a valiant way to treat brands."

"You have to love your brand before your customers will," said Paul. "You mentioned something to that effect earlier. I think I know what I need to do when I get back."

"I think you do, too," agreed Daphne. "I also think you knew before you went on this press tour that your goose was sort of cooked. When did you know?"

Paul looked anxiously at the gathering passengers, still awaiting the signal to board. "The energy on the team was never right. We were basking in the glow of *Ethereal Gaze*. We never let go of it and started again from scratch. We were on autopilot, allowing ourselves to be deluded."

"So the big difference between one and two wasn't so much the product as the process," summarized Daphne. "The first process embodied radiance, so the end result was radiance. The second was so-so, thus the product never climbed much beyond mediocrity. If the journey isn't significant, how can the landing place be significant?"

Paul noticed that some of the stalled passengers at the gate were beginning to listen to Daphne, causing him to speak more softly. "Yeah, I guess I knew that for some time. I wanted to wish that away. Instead I let myself fall into the trap of the one-hit wonders."

"Not just yet, Paul. I want you to think about one more thing. Do you remember when we first started talking this evening, way back, hours ago, I asked you a question." She had lowered her voice as well.

"You asked me a lot of questions tonight. I have a ton of notes. I'll be writing down a lot more when I get to my seat. I would have to look back."

"One of the first things I asked you was what was different now, since your promotion to VP. What's changed in the way you approach your job, going from being a product manager to an executive?"

"Right, you did ask me that. I didn't have a very good answer."

"You didn't have any answer at all," returned Daphne. "Do you now?"

"More responsibility? More pressure? The stakes are higher? I have more to lose?"

"All of that, but something more—something much more fundamental," coached Daphne. "Are you doing or leading?"

"When I was a product manager I was doing a little of both, but mostly I was doing."

🎤 "If the journey isn't significant, how can the landing place be significant?"

"Right, you were in charge of the product, so a lot of the work you did was functional, getting things done. Now you're in charge of not only the one product, but lots of products. What else do you have to tie together these days?"

"Sales and marketing, finance, legal, human resources, administration . . . everything!" quietly roared Paul. "Stuff I know and stuff I don't. It all intersects on my desk whether I understand it or not."

"What's your day like now?" asked Daphne.

"Scattered, interrupt-driven. I have so little time to do things myself, especially the product-related stuff that got me promoted."

"How do you effectively handle that?" probed Daphne.

"I have to get my work done through others," replied Paul. "I have to leverage my time. I have to delegate."

"Much more than delegate—you have to inspire. You have to invigorate. You have to lead. That's what you have to do when you get back. That's why I asked you what was different."

"I was hoping you might forget to ask me," confessed Paul. "You're right, as usual. I played it too close to the line on this product. There were too many instances where I wasn't sure what was appropriate for me to do, and what was appropriate for me to ask others to do."

🎤 "Are you doing or leading?"

"The true struggle of leadership lives in the player-coach. You can't be too hands-on, but you can't be hands-off. They have to respect you as a doer, not a talker, but you have to get them to give all they have, so the collective power gives you exponential output, compounding results well beyond what each individual has to offer. No one can hold back, and the teamwork has to encompass an unmatchable whole. That's leading, the magic of making more happen than anyone could imagine."

"You also mentioned a pop quiz when we started talking this evening," remembered Paul. "This is the test, right?"

"Part of it," said Daphne. "You're not doing too badly at the moment. I'll email you the rest. We'll see how much you remember, how much you take to heart, how much you really want to enjoy End-less Encores."

The LCD screen above the gate signaled that Daphne's boarding group had been called. All the passengers were funneling toward the gate agent. It was time for them to separate.

"You've got to get onboard," said Paul. "You invested a lot of time in me tonight. You didn't even have to talk to me. I'm still not sure why you did that."

"Time is not endless," replied Daphne. "No matter how clever we are, we can't create more of it, only use what we have wisely. I have a particu-larly keen insight into that at the moment. This was time well spent for both of us. Lucky me, I picked the right person to hear what I had to say."

"You've been so great. I hope that the doctors give you a clear reading. You can't retire. There are so many people like me who need to hear what you have to say, to keep them from wiping out."

"I was pretty sure I was going to retire going into this," said Daphne. "You've made me think about it in a different way. There is a lot of haze in our business world. Is it failing or is it learning? That's the key to leading by example."

"Someday I may write all this down to share," said Paul. "Would that be okay?"

"You couldn't possibly make me prouder," said Daphne. "You know enough to give back."

"Promise me you won't retire," said Paul. His eyes were a little red, truly uncharacteristic of him. He had been inspired by Daphne in a way he knew he could never fully articulate, and this moment of farewell to the stranger he had met only hours ago was peculiarly overwhelming. He had been disarmed and rearmed simultaneously, but he had also been ignited, made to see the quiet power of an individual who cared so much about her teams, her customers, her mission. He was genuinely worried for her. If she couldn't go back to work, what would that mean? Maybe she didn't have much time left at all. How could she be so cheerful, so optimistic facing not only the end of her career, but possibly the end of her life? She was extraordinary, but like all human life, she was fragile. She would never show it, but time was precious for her now. Indeed that was why she had spent the entire evening

𝕌 "Is it failing or is it learning?"

talking with him about the things that mattered to her, the things she wanted to matter to others. Her manner had been casual, but each word had been carefully chosen, each idea more vital than the next. He knew she could tell he was a bit off balance, but she might have been as well.

Daphne turned the wheels on her rollaboard toward the boarding ramp ahead of her. "Like I said, my family has to come first, but I will think about it in earnest. I have to be transparent with my board of directors. Maybe they'll be understanding if the insurance premiums aren't ridiculous. Dark bunch of bean counters, those cads. Governance types can have a curious sense of humor. Let's hope my heart is stronger than some experts might currently think."

"Your heart is incredibly strong. Unbelievably strong . . . whatever comes after strong!"

"You're a good fellow, Paul. Go make things right, not just for this product launch, for the next three decades of product launches."

"Others need to hear what you have to say."

"Maybe you'll tell them for me, and add a little creativity of your own. Focus relentlessly on the extraordinary. Don't get thrown by naysayers. Mediocrity has a loathsome track record of rejecting the extraordinary for sport, even out of spite. When you lead, never settle for less than you expect of yourself. Passion for excellence is without substitute as a motivator. You can never care too much."

"You think I can pull this off?" asked Paul. "I don't have your gifts. I don't have your experience. I'm not even sure I know what it means to win."

"You know what it means to listen, so you know the clearest path forward," concluded Daphne. "You have no idea how high you are going to soar. I have excellent instincts about these things, and you will exceed my expectations."

Paul could say no more. He didn't want to let her down, but he had no idea how he would ever deliver on her prediction. She had enrolled him in a cause. His mission was now her mission. The weight with which this landed on him nearly knocked him off his feet.

They boarded the plane separately. With the additional airline status and complimentary upgrade to first class she had received, Daphne boarded first. Shortly after that, Paul crossed the ramp to the open Jetway door. Daphne was already seated when Paul boarded. She smiled but said nothing as he passed her and made his way along the center aisle to the rear of the aircraft.

Paul put his rollaboard in the overhead bin, took his seat by the window, and quickly pulled out his mobile from the canvas bag he placed under the seat in front of him. As he promised, he texted to his lead software engineer Randy, "I'm en route, Saturday Sort-Out is on, see you and the team at the office in the morning, not too early." He then powered down his mobile for takeoff and put it back in his canvas bag. He withdrew the notebook

♀ "Focus relentlessly on the extraordinary."

Daphne had given to him and began scribbling more entries in the blank pages. He wrote furiously through taxi and takeoff, trying to remember everything she had said. When the plane reached full cruising altitude, he stopped writing and slipped the notebook into his canvas bag. He stared out the portal into the dark night sky and thought about the last few hours, how astonishing they had been, what a once-in-a-lifetime classroom that airport lounge had been.

His career was not over. It was beginning. Perseverance was what mattered. There would be no such thing as failure as long as there was learning. Opportunities would come and go. There would be wins and losses, none of which he would ever be able to predict. Resilience constructed a gallant arc. The learning would always be his. No one could take that from him. Persistence was triumph. The wisdom he would apply would be his key to discovering Endless Encores.

People. Products. Profits. In that order. Yes, she was right.

There was no way she could retire. There was no way a fluctuating heartbeat was going to slow her down or stop her. She was stronger than that. She had to go on. The business world needed more people like Daphne. She had to stay in the game. That was only fair. No market forces, nothing of the unpredictable could deter the mission, the evangelism, everything that mattered most in making innovation happen.

When the flight attendant came by, Paul asked for a glass of water. He drank it without taking a breath. He wasn't sure what was happening to him, but his entire thought process had been transformed. He simply couldn't wait to get back to work on Saturday.

When they got off the plane in Los Angeles, Daphne was met by a driver with a card holding her name. She offered Paul a ride, but his car was in long-term parking. He thanked her in as few words as he could muster, but politely declined. Again she smiled. So did he. A different kind of smile. An enlightened smile. They were in a different place. The dialogue had come to a close.

Daphne and Paul shook hands and said good-bye. Paul was certain they would correspond over email going forward, but wondered if he would ever see her again. Somehow he didn't think so. She had her own concerns, some business, some personal, all significant. She had shared graciously, openly, but it was time for her to focus again on her world. He had the best of her stories and knew what he had to do. He had his own world in need of attention, and the coming test was still ahead of him.

♫ ♫ ♫

Paul's Notebook: Departing

♪ ♪ ♪

♪ Brand equity has to be nurtured through your promise.

♪ Get the process right and the product will follow.

♪ Leading by example means embodying inspiration.

♪ It's not failing if it's learning.

♪ You can never care too much.

Chapter 6: Returning

♩ ♩ ♩

Twelve years had passed. It was another foggy night in the Bay Area, and Paul found himself back in the SFO airport lounge. Despite the wonderful dialogue he had enjoyed with Daphne, ever since that unique evening so long ago he had made it a point to fly in and out of Oakland whenever he could to avoid long delays, given the smaller airport's on-time record. This Friday evening he had no choice but to connect through San Francisco and once again was victim to failed equipment on the tarmac. The delay looked to be several hours.

Strangely familiar after so much time had passed, the gated private club had been remodeled and redecorated, though much of the surroundings looked the same. Paul had just finished focus groups in Vancouver for his latest project, and while the feedback hadn't been overly exuberant, the fixes it brought to mind told him he might have another stealth winner in the pipeline. Or maybe not. At this point in his career, he never knew for sure if he had a major winner or loser until well after it went to market. All he knew was that he always went at each offering with everything he had, listened, retooled, and then hoped a bit of luck was on his side. He didn't need to win every time to stay in the game, but he did need to approach every project with the same level of energy, enthusiasm, commitment, and resolve, fully respecting his customers, fully respecting the creative process. He remembered her words: "Never settle for less than you expect of yourself." Nothing lit up a team like setting out to achieve the extraordinary.

Paul took a seat at the bar, on the corner where he had spoken with Daphne over a decade ago, in what had been her seat. Of course Daphne was not there. He had read in the *Wall Street Journal* that she had passed away about a year ago, a lengthy write-up of her unending triumphs, little mention of her equally unending mishaps. She had worked until her final day on the job, taking one more company public following a board role as Chair at SalientCorp. In the end, it was her heart that gave out, but she had kept it working in her favor far longer than she had anticipated when they first talked. Daphne had left a substantial portion of her estate to a number of non-profits, some to a homeless shelter where she volunteered, some to climate research, and a sizeable bequest to the American Heart Association.

Paul had attended her service in Silicon Valley, but spoke to no one there. He had held the notebook she gave him tightly in his hands through the hours of accolades and reminiscing, but his time with Daphne could not be summed up in a few comments. He had heard her husband say that she wouldn't have had it any other way—she

🎙 "Never settle for less than you expect of yourself."

had wanted to work every day she had remaining because the people around her mattered so much. His name was Jake. Her adult children, Erik and Audrey, were of course at the memorial, as proud of her as she was of them. Jake said that Daphne had died quietly at home one evening. "Almost no one knew of her heart condition," said Jake. "They knew her for her joy, her work ethic, her inspiration, for always giving back as generously as she could." Paul understood in depth what that meant. He sat there in mindfulness, forever changed, forever appreciative.

They had stayed in touch on and off for a few years after the evening they met. Since then, Paul had enjoyed a remarkable career trajectory, much as Daphne predicted. He hardly remembered *Ethereal Gaze 2*. As she also predicted, it had not been a disaster, just not the colossal hit he had wanted it to be, despite some significant retooling. Much to his surprise, *Ethereal Gaze 3* had been bigger than both of the first two together, a monster hit that won every award in the industry. The company had asked Paul to oversee *Ethereal Gaze 4*, but he passed. It was time for him to reinvent himself and foster a new brand.

He had left his secure job to start his own videogame production company, and after two modest successes and one noble failure, he had launched the biggest game of his career, a strategy puzzler

🎤 "They knew her for her joy, her work ethic, her inspiration, for always giving back as generously as she could."

called *Likeness of Lear* that became one of the bestselling videogames of all time and put a new brand on the map. That brought offers to sell his company, which Paul simply could not refuse. He stayed for two years after the company sale, overseeing the first sequel that sold even better than the original. After that, all the new deep-pocket owners wanted was more sequels, produced more quickly and sold at lower wholesale for higher volume, leveraging the goodwill in the brand promise that Paul's team had created. He wasn't up for that, so again he moved on.

With several career-making hits under his belt over the past fifteen years, amid innumerable other launches, Paul decided to change careers. He became CEO of a small peripherals firm called Visceral-Ties that had been teetering in the years following its launch glory, desperately in need of an innovative turnaround. He'd never really liked the handheld devices people used to play videogames, and when he was offered the opportunity to help reinvent a company that did just that, he couldn't resist. He brought along his chief technology officer, Randy, who had stayed with him through thick and thin. He also brought in Helen for this project, whom he hadn't seen in years, since she had shifted her career from art directing games to becoming a creative director for advertising. She was very good at it; her portfolio was unlike anything Paul had seen in her prior pursuits. Like Paul and his various enterprises, she had evolved into a new version of herself, much more confident and happy.

Their first handheld device as a new management team had gone to market about a year ago and sold a respectable number of units, but not enough to make the company's stock price respond. It was a solid next step on the journey, an admirable improvement in quality and customer experience, but not a leap. They had collected a lot of data from their customers though, and Paul had stumbled upon a quirky whiz kid from a community college named Jonah who was cooking up the next-gen product to leapfrog all the existing offerings. Jonah was untried and not formally trained, but he was extraordinary at industrial design and joyously indefatigable. Paul knew Jonah had a winner in him; he just didn't know when. On Jonah's application for the job at Visceral-Ties he had written the words, *"Think Different* is a Religion." That had made Paul think of Daphne and he hired Jonah instantly. The new product was in test cycle now, and with a few tweaks Paul and the team had discussed around the Vancouver sessions, the next release might be the moonshot they had hoped to create.

Daphne indeed had emailed Paul a pop quiz not long after their dialogue. It had asked him ten questions, to rate himself on each using a scale of 1 to 10. She had reminded him that 90 was an A-minus, and the world was filled with 90-percenters. On Paul's first try, he answered every question with full honesty, rating himself with precise conviction in each category. He tallied a score of 84. He was a solid B. That planted the seed in his mind that he was not likely on a path to Endless Encores.

A year later he took the quiz again and received an 89. A year later he was a 91—he had joined the world of 90-percenters! A year later a 93. Most recently he had gotten a 96. He still hoped to get to 98, an honest to goodness A-plus, but he knew in all honesty that he hadn't achieved it. Secretly he was okay with that. It gave him the bar he needed to keep reaching and trying.

As Paul recalled Daphne's test, he took in the clean but indistinct walls around him. He tried to recognize the bartender—it may have been that same guy Harold with a few extra pounds around the middle and a half-beard, but who could remember, who could tell? Sitting next to Paul at the bar was a professionally dressed woman, perhaps in her late twenties. She was staring into a glass of red wine. She began pounding on her mobile frantically, so hard that she knocked it out of her own hands. Paul watched as the phone fell hard to the polished hardwood floor. That was that. She was going to need another one.

"Damn it all," she wailed. "Now on top of everything else I need a new phone."

"Rough day?" asked Paul.

"Rough month, rough year," she said, regaining some of her composure. "Do we have to talk?"

"We don't, but if you change your mind, my name is Paul. I'm happily married, so you don't have to worry about me asking to buy you a drink."

She laughed, slightly disarmed. "Thanks for that. I don't think I could deal with anything like that right now. I'm Maia."

"Nice to meet you, Maia. I'm no genius, but I've found beating up on your phone can only fix things so much."

"I'm glad I broke it. Now my idiot boss can stop criticizing me, or at least I can pretend like she's not criticizing me until I get home and get a new one. I'm headed home to Seattle, at some point I guess. If I can get out of here, I might still be able to fix this press fiasco before the filing deadline."

Paul worked hard to choke back a smile, but she saw it anyway. "I don't mean to chuckle, but a little over a decade ago, I was sitting on the exact same barstool you are, stuck in this same airport, trying to get home to LA with a press fiasco of my own staring me down. Trust me, getting out of this airport won't be the last hurdle you face. The only thing over that hill is another hill."

"Irony is abundant," lamented Maia. "How did that delay end for you?"

"Possibly the most important night of my career. Sitting where I am was a woman named Daphne, who was CEO of a huge public company. We talked for hours. She was on her way to see a heart specialist for an unusual condition that had crept into her life. I was in the middle of a tough product release. All of her focus was on me."

"What happened to her?"

"She beat the odds, went back to work, kept inspiring people like me to do the best work of their careers. She continued working until she passed

🎤 "The only thing over that hill is another hill."

away not long ago. She loved her work, most of all the talent she assembled all around her. Her life was balanced, but she was driven to innovate in a way that is almost impossible to describe. Work mattered to her, and she wanted it to matter to the people whose lives she entered."

"She sounds amazing," said Maia. "But I doubt she could help me."

"That's what I thought," said Paul, reaching into his same well-worn canvas bag and retrieving the dog-eared notebook she had given him as a memento. "I spent most of that evening listening to her, and writing down some of her ideas in this notebook she gave me. I carry it with me wherever I go. Even made a few copies of it to keep in reserve on the off chance I lose this one."

"What's it say in the notebook?" asked Maia. "What could be so important that you'd carry it with you wherever you go?"

"I not only carry it with me, I update it all the time with new ideas I get from talking to people who inspire me, like Daphne. What's the issue with this deadline you're facing?"

"I work for a food importer that used to be pretty well-known," said Maia, handing him her business card. "If you and your wife like high-quality gourmet food from around the world, we're the best. Well, we used to be. That's why I signed on, but it's been hard to get people to listen since we started slumping. I'm afraid we might lose it all, become a footnote in foodstuff history."

"Not unfamiliar ground to me, except for the part about fine food." He took her business card and put it in his jacket pocket.

"I've known what's wrong with our product line since they hired me, and I've been waiting patiently for the chance to show them I can fix it," added Maia. "About six months ago, they put me in charge of purchasing for the fall season, but just when I placed the order, overseas commodity rates went up, skyrocketing out of nowhere. Of course that meant we had to raise prices to cover the costs. Now nothing is selling."

"Maybe you should have delayed the order until next season."

"I was trying to adjust prices without looking like we were liquidating inventory, when a popular food blog attacked us for gouging our customers, which of course we weren't. When I published that on the blogger's comment section, he said it didn't matter because the collection was so ordinary it wasn't worth half the price. We're sitting on a football field of raw materials in our warehouse and people think it's ordinary and overpriced. My boss says I have to fix it or else."

"Tough initial product release for you—you knew for sure what you wanted to bring to market, only market forces and public opinion didn't cooperate."

"Blogger opinion, and he's an idiot, too. My collection would do fine if people would just get out of my way. What would Daphne have said about that?"

"I wouldn't know. She's not with us anymore so it would be conjecture. I would say just because you thought you knew the answer to a problem, your knowledge alone probably won't let you solve the problem. What gets you this far can also take you down. You might be missing a few pieces. Rally a little support around what you believe so deeply, find out what's evading you."

"It's not that simple. Every business is different."

"Those idiotic people you want to get out of the way, they're your customers and stakeholders. You're going to have to get them on your side, not drive them into the hills."

"Daphne taught you that?" asked Maia.

"She taught me how to stay out of the Dead Brand Graveyard. It pretty much worked. We have a little time on our hands. Would you like me to take you through a few of her ideas?"

"Maybe, but what's the most important lesson you've learned since that conversation with Daphne a decade ago?" asked Maia.

"I can boil that down to three words if you like, in a moment. I'd like to hear a little more about how your business works before I say too much. Daphne was all about process, going slow to go fast, getting to action and results through strategy and vision, learning and listening."

"Just three words?" questioned Maia. "I'm not sure I get it."

🎤 "What gets you this far can also take you down."

"I didn't either," said Paul. "It took years. Maybe your food line wasn't as special as you thought. Maybe you didn't corral enough talent, or have a clear brand promise, or, in your case, have the right business model. The same trick seldom works twice. I've found that a small twist on the same concept that put you on the map has an extremely low likelihood of delighting your customers. Trying to repeat a big success with more of the same is one of the riskiest strategies you can pursue, and yet, that's where the people behind your curtain will so often push you."

"My boss wants certainty in creativity," noted Maia.

"No such thing. Otherwise they wouldn't pay us to do what we do. As long as the work is harder than what a computer can solve, we have some job security. One of the first things Daphne asked me was if I liked music. She was quite the fan of Paul McCartney. Do you have a favorite artist?"

Before Maia could answer, she heard some rumbling in the room and looked up at the flight board above the bar. Her flight had flickered from red to green. It was departing after all.

"I guess I'm not going to be able to hear the rest of the story," said Maia.

"My loss," uttered Paul.

"I hope your flight gets out of here early as well."

🎤 "The same trick seldom works twice."

"I'm okay," expressed Paul. "Strangely, this place sits well with me, delays included."

Maia got up and headed for the door, then looked back at Paul. She called to him across the room. "Any chance you'd be willing to send me a copy of that notebook? I'll reimburse you for the postage."

"I have your card. I'll send one along. If any of it inspires you, we can talk another time."

Maia smiled and dashed out the door toward the concourse. As she did, the bartender looked over at him. He seemed to recognize Paul's voice.

"I know you, don't I?" said the bartender.

"I think you offered me two hundred dollars for this notebook once," cited Paul.

"Daphne's friend," acknowledged Harold-the-bartender. It was him after all. "How about a scotch on the house in Daphne's memory? Maybe you'll send me a copy of that notebook, too?"

"It would be my honor," affirmed Paul.

Harold reached for the top shelf. He poured it in a crystal glass and pushed it across the bar. Paul looked to the empty seat next to him, where he'd sat so long ago, took a sip, and grinned. He opened his notebook and jotted down a few more ideas. He knew the notebook would never be complete, no more than the process of reinvention would ever be complete.

Paul couldn't wait to get back to work. One project was being honed, and another project was about to begin. Hits? Misses? Who knew? All that mattered was that he believed in the creative process. He loved innovating all the time. He believed in the team. He believed in the project plan. He believed in the business model. He believed in passing along the knowledge.

As Paul took in all the somber background grumbling around him, he looked up from his notebook and glass to see that Maia had returned. He was a bit surprised, but not really.

"False positive?" asked Paul. "Equipment failure or fog?"

"I rebooked to a later flight," replied Maia. "Risky, huh, with all these flights being cancelled?"

"Need a little closure?" inquired Paul. "Have a seat. The bartender here knows what he's doing."

"I hope this won't take long, but you didn't tell me the three words that will save my career," said Maia.

"People, Products, Profits—in that order."

"Oh come on, it can't be that simple," responded Maia.

"I hope you have a few hours," said Paul. "There's nothing simple about it."

♪ ♪ ♪

Paul's Notebook: Returning

♫ ♫ ♫

♪ Passion for achieving the outrageous is unstoppable.

♪ Share kindly what you learn and give back without reservation.

♪ Volatility is the norm.

♪ Our greatest strengths are our greatest weaknesses.

♪ Force yourself beyond your comfort zone.

Epilogue: The Pop Quiz

♩ ♩ ♩

Dear Paul:

As much as an airport delay is hardly something to celebrate, I think the conversation we had last month might prove that otherwise. I wanted to give you a chance to digest all that and see if you could get your lackluster product in better shape before I distracted you with this email.

You asked me if there would be a test, and there is. It takes place every single day you recommit to your work, but on your request I pulled together a condensed version for you below, ten simple questions that summarize all of what we discussed. If you want to know if you have a chance at building a sustainable process of reinvention, in essence what you might consider a brand, answer the following questions honestly on a scale of 1 to 10, where 1 is Not at All and 10 is All In.

A grade of much less than 90% means you could be on course to being a one-hit wonder. A grade of 100% means you very well could have a chance at a lifelong career of wins and losses, where the wins pay for the losses. No, you can't afford to be a 90-percenter on any of these. You really can't.

Take your time thinking about these. There really is no rush. You needn't show the answers to anyone but yourself, but you'll only find useful guidance on where you might want to focus if you are completely honest. There are no trick questions, but for me every one matters. If you have that spiral notebook I gave you and you filled with ideas, now might be a good time to pull it out and cram. As far as I'm concerned, this is completely an open-book test, as long as you are entirely honest in how you score your answers:

1) Do you have a mission that is more than words?

2) Do you work by the values you identify?

3) Do you revere talent and creativity?

4) Do you eat your own dog food?

5) Do you seek authentic feedback?

6) Do you reject the notion that "good enough" is okay for primetime?

7) Do you cannibalize your own markets before the competition does it for you?

8) Do you acknowledge your customer as The Boss?

9) Do you have a business plan that you understand?

10) Do you have a brand promise that you love?

Retake this quiz anytime you're feeling like you're in a funk, or your creativity has stalled, or your team is on a path to the ordinary. At the very least take it once a quarter. You'll find that if your score has slipped you'll know how to get back on track, and if your score is up you might be on the verge of the next big thing coming to market.

By the way, you convinced me to stay in the game. Nobody's counting me out, not as long as there are people I meet who are committed to making the business world more human, more lasting, more innovative, and more fun.

Always your fan,
Daphne

♩ ♩ ♩

Appendix: Paul McCartney Set List

♩ ♩ ♩

In the spirit of pure aspiration, I include here the set list that Paul McCartney and his band played at Dodger Stadium on August 10, 2014. He was seventy-two years old at the time. I was fortunate to attend that concert, perhaps the ninth or tenth time I have seen Paul play live, dating back to the mid-1970s. I include the original release year of each of the songs to the best of my imperfect research, simply to illustrate what a long, exemplary career of *Endless Encores* could look like. Paul contributed to all of these songs from full or shared composition to recording to performing, and while he would likely be the first to acknowledge the teamwork in the creative process of each, it is clear that he is the driver behind this manifest of *Endless Encores*. I don't think many of us are likely to have a résumé that looks like this, but it's good to know that it's possible!

1) "Eight Days a Week" (1964)

2) "Save Us" (2013)

3) "All My Loving" (1963)

4) "Listen to What the Man Said" (1975)

5) "Let Me Roll It" (1973)

6) "Paperback Writer" (1966)

7) "My Valentine" (2012)

8) "Nineteen Hundred and Eighty-Five" (1974)

9) "The Long and Winding Road" (1970)

10) "Maybe I'm Amazed" (1970)

11) "I've Just Seen a Face" (1965)

12) "We Can Work It Out" (1965)

13) "Another Day" (1971)

14) "And I Love Her" (1964)

15) "Blackbird" (1968)

16) "Here Today" (1982)

17) "New" (2013)

18) "Queenie Eye" (2013)

19) "Lady Madonna" (1968)

20) "All Together Now" (1968)

21) "Lovely Rita" (1967)

22) "Everybody Out There" (2013)

23) "Eleanor Rigby" (1966)

24) "Being for the Benefit of Mr. Kite!" (1967)

25) "Something" (1969)

26) "Ob-La-Di, Ob-La-Da" (1968)

27) "Band on the Run" (1974)

28) "Back in the U.S.S.R." (1968)

29) "Let It Be" (1970)

30) "Live and Let Die" (1973)

31) "Hey Jude" (1968)

32) "Day Tripper" (1965)

33) "Hi, Hi, Hi" (1972)

34) "I Saw Her Standing There" (1963)

35) "Yesterday" (1965)

36) "Helter Skelter" (1968)

37) "Golden Slumbers" (1969)

38) "Carry That Weight" (1969)

39) "The End" (1969)

Reference Sources: Liner notes on the various albums; www.Setlist.FM, *Beatles Complete* © 1976 Warner Bros Publications.

♫ ♫ ♫

Acknowledgments and Grace

♫ ♫ ♫

There are always so many people to thank on a project like this, all of them names that mean the world to me and likely little to those who scan this page. It's kind of like a college scholarship award or the marquee on a building named for someone a hundred years ago—you wonder if the person was real. I promise you, the people I name who help me are very real.

My wife, Shelley, makes everything possible. I can't say any more about her than I did in the dedication to my first book, except to say she did it again. She got me through another one. I'm not sure how she does it, but she is a bastion of optimism and encouragement. Her authenticity and natural candor cause me to rethink the world every day. I only hope you are as lucky as I am to have a life partner who believes in you when you most and least need it. If you don't, keep looking. Shelley will tell you, it will happen.

Lou Aronica, my editor and publisher, has made my life immeasurably better. He has given me the confidence to believe I should continue typing words, and that helps me more than he will ever know. He once worked for a publisher that had a moonshot with an early business parable, so when I asked him if this was a worthwhile pursuit, it was not a rhetorical question. He gave me one bit of warning and one bit of reinforcement that made me think carefully about each word in this short work. He said don't underestimate how difficult it is to write simply when you have something important you want to convey, that many of these business books are rotten because the authors take their readers for granted. He then told me he was certain I wouldn't do that because I would consider each idea from experience, and then craft each word as the voice of my heart.

A couple of decades ago, I worked for three years for a boss named Harry Wilker. He was one of a very few bosses who made me both a better worker and a better person. We didn't have much time together, our business was fast-moving and changed quickly under our feet, but every moment mattered. Oh, did I learn from Harry, so much of what is here, not the least of which was the true meaning of the oft-repeated phrase, "Projects are always short, careers may or may not be long—your choice." He also told me that I would forget most of the details around even the most impassioned projects I would pursue over the years, especially the most awful ones, but if I was doing it right, I would remember the people, especially the good ones. He was right.

Doug Carlston, who was the founder and CEO of Broderbund when I joined that company, had hired Harry Wilker, one of many gifts he gave to me. Doug talked about how the world was filled with 90-percenters the first time I had lunch with him at a nondescript café in Marin, and the last time we had lunch before saying goodbye. That was another gift I received from him. There were many more. That not-so-tiny company that could—that was, for an immeasurably brief moment, the second largest consumer software company in the world behind a more famous one in Seattle—changed my life forever. I may write about that company again. You never know.

My dad helped me learn how to sell, and that selling is a good thing if you love what you sell and forever respect your customers more than what's in a deal for you. He taught me to always leave a little money on the table if it means building trust, and that trust is a global currency with unlimited renewable dividends both extrinsic and intrinsic. He also taught me that a customer relationship by definition is long term.

I dedicated this book to Father David Coon, who was headmaster of Iolani School, where someday the notes and such for these books I write will be archived. When the words "Lead By Example" run through my brain, it is him that I see. He is a bastion of strength, integrity, intelligence, resilience, and love. He made everything in my life possible by causing me to see who I was long before the age of twenty. I sent him a longhand note a year ago telling him this book was dedicated in his name. He wrote back: "I look forward to your work about People, Products, and Profits. I'm trying to fit those ideas into a sermon. No luck so far."

Father Coon, I hope your luck is turning. Mine did the moment our paths intersected.

Lisa Hickey, you make The Good Men Project good, and you make me a more devoted writer. Thank you for standing tall no matter the odds.

Gene Del Vecchio, I don't think anyone has read more of the same words I have written than you, over and over. You are always there for me, and you always make me Think Different.

Kate Zentall has been an *endlessly* supportive literary colleague no matter how early or late a draft I put in front of her. She exudes taste and class, and loves language with her every breath.

My early manuscript readers were amazing in their candor and arm-wrestling over issues big and small (when you're massaging words, nothing seems small). My warmest appreciation to Michael Eisner, Mitch Dolan, Steve Parkis, Bruce Friedricks, Philip Hopbell, Clint Ivy, Jessica Ivy, Annsley Chapman Strong, Stewart Halpern, Dan Sherlock, Sabrina Roblin, Scott Freiman, Allison Fine, Barb Adams, Rachael Worby, Emily Smith, Irv Rothenberg, Christopher Keefe, Rob Myers, Scott Witt, Patricia Wilson, Amanda Silber Levitt, Mary-Margaret Walker, Becky Stein, Noah Falstein, Beth Collins Ellard, Roger Ritchie, Ron Stitt, Mark Laudenslager, and Mike Ward.

Mitchell Maxwell, Jessica Schmidt, Aaron Brown, and Hilary Sierpinski at The Story Plant, you are always in my corner, no matter what. Don't think I don't know it. Barbara Aronica-Buck, you humble me with your inspiring jacket design. Nora Tamada, my clairvoyant copy editor, I trust you with my words because you care for them as if they were your own.

My readers of the first book and all the blog reviewers who supported *This Is Rage* out of the gate, you made it okay for me to call myself an author. Without all of you I'm simply filling the ether with text blots. Writing is a dialogue, and for it to have impact there must be a circle. You are the circle, and we are in this together.

Most of all, gracious thanks to my teams over the years at Cinemaware, Philips, Disney, Broderbund, Shop.com, and now Thrift Books and The Good Men Project—all of you accidentally found yourselves in this real-time experiment. None of you were one-hit wonders. Many of you crisscrossed several journeys with me, lots of misses, but enough hits that let me say we are on the right path. Others may disagree, like the angry fund manager in Chapter 4 who stormed out of the airport lounge in disgust, sure in his own ideology that we are pudding heads. Yep, he probably has more dough than all of us combined. What we have is something else, and he'll never have it. This is ours.

Thank you so much for letting me share with you. We begin anew. I wish for you always a mind-boggling concert tour of *Endless Encores*. No way I find you in the Dead Brand Graveyard. Not a chance.

♩ ♩ ♩

Want Some More?

♪ ♪ ♪

In the Preface to this book I mentioned that a lot of the thinking shared here was worked out over time on my blog, CorporateIntel (www.CorporateIntel.us). As I also noted, my original intention was to include selections from the blog and link them with the story of Daphne and Paul, but over time I came to think of their story as a standalone parable. I figured you could always go to my blog online for free if you wanted to read more about People-Products-Profits in a nonfiction flow.

Then it occurred to me that I could easily collect a number of those blog entries and package them up for my readers, and I have done just that. If you visit my publisher's site and register for The Story Plant newsletter (www.TheStoryPlant.com), they will send you a code that will let you download a free e-book of thirty blog entries I have collected, ten each under the topics of People, Products, and Profits. These are also available online in a chronological fashion commencing in 2011, rather than sorted by topics (as we go to press, I am nearing 150 posts), but the curated collection of thirty is available exclusively to those who purchase this book and want to dig in more chapter by chapter. If you don't wish to continue to receive the newsletter from The Story Plant, you can unsubscribe at any time.

I hope you enjoy this supplemental material, which I will continue to expand in the coming years. I love to write about business practices as well as tell stories. When I can do both and share them widely, I feel like I am doing my job!

To download the collection, please visit: TheStoryPlant.com/EndlessEncores. Enter your email address when prompted.

You can also register to follow my blog at CorporateIntel.us or follow me on Twitter @CorporateIntel to receive updates as I publish new material. Just like you, my Endless Encores are meant to continue in the forever spirit of reinvention and innovation.

♩ ♩ ♩

About the Author

♩ ♩ ♩

Ken Goldstein advises start-ups and established corporations in technology, entertainment, media, and e-commerce. His current focus includes Thrift Books LLC, the largest online seller of used books in North America, and The Good Men Project, a fast-growing content site offering perspectives on social issues in the twenty-first century, where he is a frequent contributor. He publishes the business blog CorporateIntel.us and speaks frequently on the topics of creativity, innovation, and high performance teamwork.

Ken served as chief executive officer and chairman of the board of SHOP.COM, a market leader in developing creative new experiences for online consumer commerce through the convenience of OneCart®, its patented universal shopping cart. SHOP.COM was acquired by Market America, where Ken became a strategic advisor to the company's founders and senior management.

He previously served as executive vice president and managing director of Disney Online, the business unit of the Walt Disney Internet Group that produced the leading entertainment web destination for kids and families. Key achievements at Disney developed by his teams included launch of the first massively multiplayer online game for kids, *Toontown*, as well as FamilyFun.com, Movies.com, and the early broadband service Disney Connection.

Prior to Disney, Ken was vice president of entertainment at Broderbund Software and founding general manager of the company's Red Orb Entertainment division. Before the formation of Red Orb, he was responsible for all aspects of development on Broderbund's acclaimed *Carmen Sandiego* series. He also worked as a designer/producer at Philips Interactive Media and Cinemaware Corporation, and for several years as a screenwriter and television executive.

Ken and his wife Shelley, who teaches English as a Second Language, make their home in Southern California, where he is active in local government and children's welfare issues. He has served on the boards of Hathaway-Sycamores Child and Family Services, the Make-A-Wish Foundation of Greater Los Angeles, and Full Circle Programs. He received his Bachelor of Arts degree from Yale University.

His first book, *This Is Rage: A Novel of Silicon Valley and Other Madness*, was published by The Story Plant in October 2013 and adapted by the author for stage production. *Endless Encores* is his second book.

♩ ♩ ♩